25 Messianic Signs

in Israel Today

All Scripture quotations are from the King James Version of the Holy Bible.

Printed in the United States of America

ISBN 1-57558-39-X

25 Messianic Signs

in Israel Today

Dr. Noah Hutchings
with Gilla Treibich

Table of Contents

Foreword

I was honored when Rev. Hutchings turned to me to participate in the writing of a book about messianic signs. He knows what my feelings are, although we have never discussed the signs under this specific form. It has been my special privilege to guide Rev. Hutchings' trips in Israel. My knowledge of Scripture isn't nearly as broad as his; nevertheless we soon discovered we often shared an understanding of Scripture. There are, of course, differences, seeing that I am Jewish.

The state of Israel was somewhat a miracle to the Jewish people, especially after the Holocaust. In his poem "The Jewish Cemetery in Rhode Island," Longfellow wrote about Israel that "dead nations never rise again." But Israel had God's promise it would return to its land. Israel was told it would once again be a nation, and as we very well know, God keeps His promises. The Jews kept praying every year and every festival: "Next year in Jerusalem." When we returned to Zion, we felt this was the beginning of a new age. In our prayers we ask God to bless the state of Israel, which is "the beginning of the budding of our redemption." We know this is the first step toward redemption and toward the coming of Messiah. Whether you are Christian or Jewish, I hope this book helps you stay optimistic and continue to believe in God's promises.

—Gilla Treibich

Introduction

The messianic age involves a promise of God to Abraham, first stated in Genesis 12:1–3. Abraham was promised that from him would come descendants who would establish a great nation. God would bless this nation, and in turn this nation and its people would be a blessing to all nations and peoples. We later learn in the Scriptures that this promise, blessing, or covenant, would entail that this nation from Abraham would be head of all nations in this coming age in which the world would be at peace and a great King would reign over all.

This covenant, or testament, made with Abraham was inherited by the patriarch's son, Isaac, then his son, Jacob, and thence to his twelve sons. The biblical account continues to relate how Jacob's twelve sons went to Egypt to find food during a great famine. During the next four hundred years the descendants of the twelve sons of Jacob multiplied to several million. God allowed a persecution against Abraham's descendants in Egypt to arise in order that this promise to the people might be realized. God sent Moses, a descendant of Abraham, to bring the Hebrews, as they were then called, out of bondage and lead them to the land on which they were to become this nation God had promised.

After Moses led the Israelites out of Egypt into the wilderness of the Sinai desert, God gave them the Law which comprised ten definitive commandments (Exodus 20). The promises within the covenant God made with father Abraham were contingent upon Israel as a nation being able to keep every commandment. When this occurred, or came to fruition, then the Lord would reward His earthly people with the Kingdom, or messianic age. However, when Israel as a nation began to more and more repudiate the Law, or transgress the Law, the Kingdom promise would become more and more remote and judgments for their national, corporate sins would follow:

> If thou wilt not observe to do all the words of this law that are written in this book, that thou mayest fear this glorious and fearful name, THE LORD THY GOD; Then the LORD will make thy plagues wonderful, and the plagues of thy seed, even great plagues, and of long continuance, and sore sicknesses, and of long continuance. Moreover he will bring upon thee all the diseases of Egypt, which thou wast afraid of; and they shall cleave unto thee. Also every sickness, and every plague, which is not written in the book of this law, them will the LORD bring upon thee, until thou be destroyed. And ye shall be left few in number, whereas ye were as the stars of heaven for multitude; because thou wouldest not obey the voice of the LORD thy God. And it shall come to pass, that as the LORD rejoiced over you to do you good, and to multiply you; so the LORD will rejoice over you to destroy you, and to bring you to nought; and ye shall be plucked from off the land whither thou goest to possess it. And the LORD shall scatter thee among all people, from the one end of the earth even unto the other; and there thou shalt serve other gods, which neither thou nor thy fathers have known, even wood and stone. And among these nations shalt thou find no ease, neither shall the sole of thy foot have rest: but the LORD shall give thee there a trem-

> bling heart, and failing of eyes, and sorrow of mind: And thy life shall hang in doubt before thee; and thou shalt fear day and night, and shalt have none assurance of thy life: In the morning thou shalt say, Would God it were even! and at even thou shalt say, Would God it were morning! for the fear of thine heart wherewith thou shalt fear, and for the sight of thine eyes which thou shalt see. And the LORD shall bring thee into Egypt again with ships, by the way whereof I spake unto thee, Thou shalt see it no more again: and there ye shall be sold unto your enemies for bondmen and bondwomen, and no man shall buy you.
>
> —Deuteronomy 28:58–68

Israel occupied the land of promise under a system of theocratic-democracy, also called the "time of the judges," for approximately four hundred years (1400 B.C. to 1000 B.C.). After the death of King Solomon, the nation split into two parts: the northern kingdom, composed of ten tribes, and retaining the name Israel; and the southern kingdom, composed of two tribes, Judah and Benjamin, taking the name of the larger tribe, Judah. The citizens of Judah became identified as Jews.

Just as Israel had been governed under the judges for a period of about four hundred years, under the theocratic-autocracy reign of the kings, from Saul to Zedekiah, the last king of Judah, was also a period of about four hundred years. Forty is the biblical number of testing or trial, and ten is the biblical number for finality, proof, or completion. Therefore, Israel was tried in Egypt for four hundred years, under the judges for four hundred years, under the kings for four hundred years, and from the return from Babylon to the destruction of Jerusalem and the Temple was approximately four hundred years. Five is the biblical number of grace or divine favor, and during the church age, also referred to as the dispensation of grace, Israel was dispersed from the land for approximately two thousand years, or five times four hundred.

As the northern kingdom became more engrossed in idol worship, God allowed Assyria to conquer Israel and ravage the people and the land. The year was 720 B.C. As the southern kingdom also violated the commandments of the Law and the kings became utterly corrupt (2 Kings 24), God failed to deliver Judah from the invading Babylonians. In 600 B.C. King Jehoiakim surrendered Jerusalem to Nebuchadnezzar.

While the Assyrian and Babylonian wars with resulting periods of devastation and captivity were vicious and horrible periods for Israel, all the prophets from Moses to Malachi were given revelations concerning an even greater time of judgment, persecution, and dispersion. This period would be longer and the people of Israel would be scattered into all nations, the entire world, not just Assyria or Babylon.

What concerned the prophets of Israel most was: When would this period end? When would God keep His promises to Israel? When would the Lord take away the iniquity of Israel so that the messianic age of peace, plenty, and righteousness would be realized?

Just as Moses was given the vision of Israel's dispersion and persecution, the prophet was also given the assurance that God would keep His promises:

> And it shall come to pass, when all these things are come upon thee, the blessing and the curse, which I have set before thee, and thou shalt call them to mind among all the nations, whither the LORD thy God hath driven thee, And shalt return unto the LORD thy God, and shalt obey his voice according to all that I command thee this day, thou and thy children, with all thine heart, and with all thy soul; That

> then the LORD thy God will turn thy captivity, and have compassion upon thee, and will return and gather thee from all the nations, whither the LORD thy God hath scattered thee. If any of thine be driven out unto the outmost parts of heaven, from thence will the LORD thy God gather thee, and from thence will he fetch thee: And the LORD thy God will bring thee into the land which thy fathers possessed, and thou shalt possess it; and he will do thee good, and multiply thee above thy fathers. And the LORD thy God will circumcise thine heart, and the heart of thy seed, to love the LORD thy God with all thine heart, and with all thy soul, that thou mayest live. And the LORD thy God will put all these curses upon thine enemies, and on them that hate thee, which persecuted thee. And thou shalt return and obey the voice of the LORD, and do all his commandments which I command thee this day. And the LORD thy God will make thee plenteous in every work of thine hand, in the fruit of thy body, and in the fruit of thy cattle, and in the fruit of thy land, for good: for the LORD will again rejoice over thee for good, as he rejoiced over thy fathers: If thou shalt hearken unto the voice of the LORD thy God, to keep his commandments and his statutes which are written in this book of the law, and if thou turn unto the LORD thy God with all thine heart, and with all thy soul.
>
> —Deuteronomy 30:1–10

Over and over in the great prophetic chapters of Daniel, the prophet pleads for understanding as to how long it would be until God's promises to Israel were realized. Over and over Daniel pleaded for God's forgiveness for his people so that the messianic age would come. In chapters two, five, seven, nine, and twelve, Daniel is informed repeatedly what would come to pass before the Messiah would come and the kingdom promised by the Lord would arrive. Daniel did not understand fully as he looked into the future, but we can understand now because we are at the end looking back.

Prophecies relating to the Messiah and His Kingdom begin at Genesis 3:16, and throughout the Old Testament there are hundreds and thousands of references to the promised messianic age. However, these promises are divided by a period called the breach: "Moreover the light of the moon shall be as the light of the sun, and the light of the sun shall be sevenfold, as the light of seven days, in the day that the LORD bindeth up the breach of his people, and healeth the stroke of their wound" (Isaiah 30:26).

References to this prophetic event were also made by Joel, Jesus, the apostle Peter, the apostle John, and others, but every reference has an end-time, messianic setting. Some Christian theologians place the beginning of the breach between God and Israel at the crucifixion of Jesus Christ; others at the destruction of the Temple and Jerusalem in A.D. 70. Within the breach is the Diaspora where the only prophecy relevant is the scattering of Israel into all nations, and descriptions of their sorrow, travail, and persecution. But on the near side of the breach with the refounding of Israel as a nation are scores of messianic prophecies, both in the Old Testament and the New Testament. For example, we read in Ezekiel 38:8:

> After many days thou shalt be visited: in the latter years thou shalt come into the land that is brought back from the sword, [and is] gathered out of many people, against the mountains of Israel, which have been always waste: but it is brought forth out of the nations, and they shall dwell safely all of them.

This prophecy relates to Israel after the nation has been refounded. It is about an invasion from the north with an alliance of Arab nations. We also read in Joel 2:30–32; 3:1–2:

> And I will shew wonders in the heavens and in the earth, blood, and fire, and pillars of smoke. The sun shall be turned into darkness, and the moon into blood, before the great and the terrible day of the LORD come. And it shall come to pass, that whosoever shall call on the name of the LORD shall be delivered: for in mount Zion and in Jerusalem shall be deliverance, as the LORD hath said, and in the remnant whom the LORD shall call. For, behold, in those days, and in that time, when I shall bring again the captivity of Judah and Jerusalem, I will also gather all nations, and will bring them down into the valley of Jehoshaphat, and will plead with them there for my people and for my heritage Israel, whom they have scattered among the nations, and parted my land.

Here again we see end-time messianic prophecies relating directly to Israel. To go through the Bible and separate the messianic prophecies in their relation to the far side or the near side of the breach would be a large book in itself.

The end-time prophecies of Jesus in the Olivet Discourse are related to Jerusalem, Israel, and the Jews:

> And they shall fall by the edge of the sword, and shall be led away captive into all nations: and Jerusalem shall be trodden down of the Gentiles, until the times of the Gentiles be fulfilled. And there shall be signs in the sun, and in the moon, and in the stars; and upon the earth distress of nations, with perplexity; the sea and the waves roaring; Men's hearts failing them for fear, and for looking after those things which are coming on the earth: for the powers of heaven shall be shaken.
>
> —Luke 21:24–26

The apostle Paul, a student of the great Jewish professor and lawyer Gamaliel, pointed to a basic messianic prophecy for Christian consideration in Romans 11:25–27:

> For I would not, brethren, that ye should be ignorant of this mystery, lest ye should be wise in your own conceits; that blindness in part is happened to Israel, until the fulness of the Gentiles be come in. And so all Israel shall be saved: as it is written, There shall come out of Sion the Deliverer, and shall turn away ungodliness from Jacob: For this is my covenant unto them, when I shall take away their sins.

The apostle Paul again referred to the resumption of worship services in the Temple at the time the Antichrist will commit the abomination of desolation (referred to several times by Daniel) as a sign of the literal coming of Christ (Messiah) and the translation of the Church.

James, the half-brother of Jesus, referred to the bringing in of the promised Davidic kingdom after the translation of the church in Acts 15:14–16. And while the judgments of the coming Tribulation period described in graphic detail in the Revelation is worldwide in scope, still in the eye of the storm we find Israel and the Law.

Without Israel or the Jew, there would be no reason for a Millennium, or Kingdom age. On the other hand, if there is to be no Millennium, there would be no reason for the Jew in the world today. Likewise, those who propose covenant theology, or replacement theology, would be right and there would be no reason for this book.

However, if we find today in Israel the end-time messianic prophecies in evidence, then we have sound reasons to believe that we are right—there will be a messianic Israel.

Sign Number One

Israel's Fig Tree

If we were to list all the signs in the Bible identifiable with the last days, latter years, or Kingdom of Heaven in order of importance, we would have to place the return of the remnant of Israel and refounding of the nation as number one.

In numerous scriptures trees are used as symbols or examples of nations. In the ninth chapter of Judges we read where the trees in due time determined to anoint a king, or one specific tree, over them. The first tree that was approached with the offer of the kingdom was the "olive tree," symbolic of spiritual Israel under the judges: "The Lord called thy name, A green olive tree . . ." (Jeremiah 11:16).

According to Judges 9:8, the olive tree was unwilling or unable to fulfill its calling and appointment. Next, we read that the trees counseled and called for the fig tree to accept the position and bring in the kingdom, but the fig tree also was unwilling or unable to accept. After the era of the judges, Israel said, "Anoint us a king," so the fig tree represented national Israel under the era of the kings. Israel is referred to in many scriptures as God's fig tree (Joel 1:7; Jeremiah 8:13; etc.). However, we read in Judges 9:11 that the fig tree was either unable or unwilling to serve as ruler over the nations, representative of the Kingdom age.

Next, the trees ask the lowly grape vine to be the ruler over the nations, but even the vine was so self-centered it would not serve in a kingdom position. The vine is symbolic of messianic Israel, the four hundred years after the prophet Malachi when a forerunner of the Messiah would appear to prepare his way (Malachi 3:1). The prophet Zechariah also referenced the coming Messiah as "The BRANCH" (Zechariah 6:12). Jesus fully understood that He was offering Himself to Israel as the Messiah when He stated in John 15:1, "I am the true vine. . . ." But the citizens of Israel said of Jesus, "We will not have this man to reign over us." (Luke 19:14).

According to the Abrahamic covenant, Israel is to be head of all nations, so finally the nations looked to Israel and concluded the only candidate left to consider was the abominable bramble bush:

> Then said all the trees unto the bramble, Come thou, and reign over us. And the bramble said unto the trees, If in truth ye anoint me king over you, then come and put your trust in my shadow: and if not, let fire come out of the bramble, and devour the cedars of Lebanon.
>
> —Judges 9:14–15

In the parable of the trees it is evident that the "bramble bush" represents the false messiah, also referred to as the coming Antichrist, or anti-Messiah. The prophet Daniel referred to the "abomination of desolation" repeatedly; Jesus, Paul, and John in the New Testament referenced the prophecy by Daniel. The false messiah presents himself as the true Messiah, and when the world does not universally worship him as God, the fires of desolation follow. The cedars of Lebanon will be burned up (Jeremiah. 22:7), Egypt will desolated for forty years and, according to Revelation, one-third of the trees will be burned up and all grass.

During the Diaspora, the Olive Tree has been cut down,

but the roots of an olive tree never die. According to Romans 11, when the church age expires, Israel will be grafted back into the roots. In Israel today the dormant vine of messianic expectations is again putting forth new branches, and the fig tree, representative of national Israel, has budded again.

In looking forward to coming judgments against his nation, Jeremiah prophesied:

> . . . therefore shall they fall among them that fall: **in the time of their visitation** they shall be cast down, saith the LORD. I will surely consume them, saith the LORD: there shall be no grapes on the vine, nor figs on the fig tree, and the leaf shall fade; and the things that I have given them shall pass away from them.
>
> —Jeremiah 8:12–13

Jesus proposed that the time of this desolation would begin with Him:

Fig trees grow in abundance in Israel

> For the days shall come upon thee, that thine enemies shall cast a trench about thee, and compass thee round, and keep thee in on every side, And shall lay thee even with the ground, and thy children within thee; and they shall not leave in thee one stone upon another; because **thou knewest not the time of thy visitation.**
>
> —Luke 19:43–44

There are two seasons of figs in Israel. As brought out by the *Fausset Bible Dictionary and Encyclopedia,* the winter figs ripen at about the time of the Passover. The leaves on the fig trees are just beginning to appear as the figs become sweet enough to eat. The fall figs ripen at about the time of Yom Kippur, and the second crop is the sweetest and more abundant harvest.

When Jesus came to Jerusalem, He stayed at the home of Mary, Martha, and Lazarus in Bethany. He would go over the Mount of Olives, through the Kidron Valley, and enter the city through one of the gates on the east wall.

The Mount of Olives is not only known for the olive trees that have historically grown on it, but also for the fig trees. Between Bethany and Jerusalem on the Mount of Olives lies a small village called Beit Pagi, which is known to Christians as Beth Page. *Pagi* in Hebrew are the young, unripe figs. This is definitely an indication for fig trees that grew and still grow on the mountain.

During the week before His crucifixion, Jesus daily traveled from Bethany to Jerusalem, and we read of one event that involved figs in Matthew 21:18–20:

> Now in the morning as he returned into the city, he hungered. And when he saw a fig tree in the way, he came to it, and found nothing thereon, but leaves only, and said unto

> it, Let no fruit grow on thee henceforward for ever. And presently the fig tree withered away. And when the disciples saw it, they marvelled, saying, How soon is the fig tree withered away!

It was not time for the fig tree to be fully leaved, but even so, it should have been heavy with sweet fruit. In this object lesson Jesus was evidently teaching the disciples by example that Israel was lacking in spiritual maturity for the Kingdom age. Fig leaves, as in the example of Adam and Eve, are representative of self-righteousness (Isaiah 64:6). The fulfillment of this prophecy in type occurred in A.D. 70.

However, this one example in no way supports covenant theology or replacement theology, to wit that the church has forever replaced Israel as God's earthly people. Jesus later taught within the context of the Olivet Discourse:

> Now learn a parable of the fig tree; When his branch is yet tender, and putteth forth leaves, ye know that summer is nigh: So likewise ye, when ye shall see all these things, know that it is near, even at the doors.
>
> —Matthew 24:32–33

The primary concern of the disciples was the restoration of the kingdom of Israel and the fulfillment of the messianic promises (Acts 1:6). Messianic concerns were also addressed by Jesus to John the Baptist. In the Olivet Discourse Jesus referred to the prophecies given Daniel, and then added others as signs in the church age, the primary one being the budding of the fig tree, the rebirth of the nation of Israel as the budding of a tender branch. The fig trees in Israel are budding, putting on fruit again, and some growing to thirty or even forty feet high. The sign of the fig tree is also coming to pass in that Israel has once more become a nation, holding forth a promise of the soon arrival of the Kingdom age.

■ ■ ■ ■ ■

The physical fig trees today in Israel are phenomenal. They are growing everywhere and producing excellent, sweet fruit. In contrast, those who came to Israel in the last century, when the land of Israel was but a subject of dreams for the Jews, found mostly desolation. Mark Twain, who came to Palestine in 1869, gives us in his book Innocents Abroad *the firsthand impressions of a traveler:*

> *For all the lands there are for dismal scenery, I think Palestine must be the prince. The hills are barren, they are dull of color, they are unpicturesque in shape. The valleys are unsightly deserts fringed with a feeble vegetation that has an expression about it being sorrowful and despondent. The Dead Sea and the Sea of Galilee sleep in the midst of a vast stretch of hill and plain wherein the eye rests upon no pleasant tint, no striking object, no soft picture dreaming in a purple haze or mottled with the shadows of the clouds. Every outline is harsh, every feature is distinct, there is no perspective—distance works no enchantment here. It is a hopeless, dreary, heartbroken land.*

The fig tree now grows again throughout Israel. It grows on the mountains of Samaria, on the mountains of Judea, and just about everywhere. The figs are of unusual size, quantity, and quality. Of course, the prophecy of Jeremiah had an initial reference to the return after the Babylonian captivity, but it also was a reference to the return of the Jews and the refounding of Israel as a nation in the twentieth century. The fig tree once again growing in Israel in such splendor and abundance, in conjunction with the return of the Jew, certainly speaks to the Jew of messianic expectations. It stands as a reminder that the land of Israel responds to the Jewish people; they alone can turn it into "a land flowing with milk and honey." When the Jews are away, Israel becomes "a land that eateth its inhabitants."

—Gilla

THE PALESTINE POST

INCORPORATING The Palestine Bulletin

IX. No. 2379. JERUSALEM, WEDNESDAY, MARCH 15, 1933. (Adar 17, 5693 — Zu (a) l Qadeh 18, 1351.)

JEWS FLEE NAZIS' REIGN OF TERROR

LONDON HEARS OF APPALLING PERSECUTIONS AND ANTI-JEWISH MEASURES

MAX REINHARDT FORCED TO FLEE

THE PALESTINE POST

JERUSALEM, SUNDAY, OCTOBER 29, 1933. (Hshvan 9, 5694 — Ragha'b 11, 1352.)

ARAB DEMONSTRATIONS CAUSE MANY FATALITIES

Violence And Bloodshed In Jaffa, Haifa, Nablus

OFFICIAL STATEMENTS

DEATH TOLL MAY MOUNT TO FIFTEEN

THE PALESTINE POST

JERUSALEM MONDAY, MAY 20, 1935. VOL. XI. No. 2635. PRICE TEN MILS

"Lawrence of Arabia" Dead

The End of a Legendary Figure

Sign Number Two

The Surety of the Return

The compilers of the Psalms, every major prophet, and a majority of the minor prophets foretold the return of the Jews from **all** nations as a prelude to the messianic age. Some theologians, as we have noted, made the church Israel during the Dark Ages and the Middle Ages in order to try to explain why there was no nation of Israel. But James, the brother of Jesus according to the flesh, wrote:

> Be patient therefore, brethren, unto the coming of the Lord. Behold, the husbandman waiteth for the precious fruit of the earth, and hath long patience for it, until he receive the early and latter rain.
>
> —James 5:7

Many Christian scholars down through the centuries of the church age became impatient and presented the explanation that the church was going to bring in the Kingdom without Israel. Moses prophesied: ". . . then the LORD thy God . . . will return and gather thee from all the nations, whither the LORD thy God hath scattered thee" (Deuteronomy 30:3). Ezekiel prophesied:

> And I will bring you out from the people, and will gather you out of the countries wherein ye are scattered, with a

> mighty hand, and with a stretched out arm, and with fury poured out.
>
> —Ezekiel 20:34

Jesus prophesied:

> And they shall fall by the edge of the sword, and shall be led away captive into all nations: and Jerusalem shall be trodden down of the Gentiles, until the times of the Gentiles be fulfilled.
>
> —Luke 21:24

Moses prophesied of Jacob and the descendants of his twelve sons: "As an eagle stirreth up her nest, fluttereth over her young, spreadeth abroad her wings, taketh them, beareth them on her wings" (Deuteronomy 32:11). While this scripture relating to the Lord's protection of His own can be claimed by Christians, it applies directly to Israel. An eagle, like most birds, will stir up the nest, throw out the feathers, and make it uncomfortable so that the young birds will learn to fly on their own. As Moses prophesied in Deuteronomy 28, during the Diaspora God has never allowed the Jews to become secure and comfortable. Books would be required to account the wanderings and persecu-

The Western-Wall, sometimes called the Wailing Wall

tions of the Jews after the destruction of Jerusalem and the Temple in A.D. 70.

Tens of thousands of Jews perished in the Roman siege of Jerusalem. Tens of thousands of the young and healthy were sold in the slave markets of Alexandria as Moses prophesied (Deuteronomy 28:68). According to Josephus, as many as five hundred Jews a day were crucified before the walls of Jerusalem to make the defenders of the city surrender. After A.D. 70 some Jews did remain in the land and others returned in the times between periods of persecutions. However, after the Bar Kochba rebellion in A.D. 132, a new era of Roman persecution began. Even so, in the sixth century, forty-three communities continued to exist in Israel (*Holy War for the Promised Land,* p. 56). One report indicates that even Mohammed led savage raids against Jewish settlements in the Negev. The Byzantines continued Jewish persecutions, and in the seventh century Muslims invaded Israel and erected a Muslim shrine on the Temple Mount. For the next thousand years Mongol armies, Muslim armies, the Crusaders from Europe, and finally Turkish armies waged wars over Israel with the remaining Jews caught in the middle. At the time Christopher Columbus sailed for America, the Spanish Inquisition, a time of intense Jewish persecution, was in progress. During the Middle Ages Jews changed their attire to that of the upper middle class in order to escape persecution. Today in Israel some of the Orthodox still wear the black coats and hats even during the summer months, a leftover tradition from the Eastern European period of Jewish persecution.

In the 1930s a new era of Jewish persecution began in Germany. The March 15, 1933, edition of the *Palestine Post* carried the headline, "JEWS FLEE NAZIS' REIGN OF TERROR." The story continued to relate that the bodies of Jews in the Berlin canals were clogging the waterways. This was

THE PALESTINE POST

Vol. IX No. 2379. JERUSALEM, WEDNESDAY, MARCH 15, 1933 (Adar 17k, 5693—Zu (a) 1 Qadeh 18, 1351)

JEWS FLEE NAZIS' REIGN OF TERROR

LONDON HEARS OF APPALLING PERSECUTIONS AND ANTI-JEWISH MEASURES

MAX REINHARDT FORCED TO FLEE

Berlin, Tuesday—London newspapers describing the appalling anti-Semitic Nazi reign of terror, declares that the bodies of Jews are daily recovered from the Spree, the Berlin canal.

Nazis in Koeln have ordered the immediate suspension of Jewish slaughter houses, confiscating all ritual appurtenances and driving Jewish butchers from the market.

Jacob Leshchinsky, who was arrested on Saturday, was released today and ordered to leave the country by Thursday.

Political police raided the Jewish Telegraphic Agency office here, finding nothing of an incriminating nature in an hour and a half search. Normal work has been resumed by the news agency.

Max Reinhardt, the famous theatrical producer, it is reported, has fled to Vienna.

Appeal to Polish Government

Warsaw, Tuesday—2,000 Polish Jews living in Saxony have requested the Polish Government to grant them passports, to enable them to leave Germany.

More than a hundred Leipzig Jews have already crossed the German border to enter Poland. So far, more than five hundred Polish Jewish families have reentered their native country.

Republican Flag Definitely Discarded

Berlin, Monday—The Republican black, red and gold flag has been discarded. The old Imperial black, white and red has been restored as national colours by a Presidential decree. This was announced by Herr Hitler by broadcast. The Swastika flag shares full equality with the Imperial flag and will be flown simultaneously on public buildings.

Herr Hitler described the flag order as "symbolic of the marriage of tradition and the young national revolution." He has commanded all public buildings in Germany to fly both flags for three days.

The Imperial Prussian flags were flying in Berlin on Sunday as a sign of mourning for Germany's war dead, memorial services for whom were held throughout Germany. President Hindenburg in the uniform of a Field-Marshal with Herr Hitler, and other Ministers took the salute of the Reichswehr, Steel Helmets and Nazi Storm Troopers after the memorial service in the Opera House of Berlin.

Nazi Chancellor Against Terrorism

Herr Hitler again has sternly warned his followers to refrain from terrorism. He says that the Nazi victory is so overwhelming that they "cannot stoop to take petty revenge." It was their task to restore a feeling of absolute security in the interests of the people, and especially for business. "Only when our enemies commit acts of violence will you be commissioned to smash resistance ruthlessly."

And "Unknowns" Shoot Down Solicitor

Herr Kiels Spiegel, a well known solicitor, who acted for the German Socialist party in countless political lawsuits was shot dead at his home at 2 a.m., on Sunday, by what the police describe as "unknown" assailants.

French Alarmed by Nazi Invasion of Demilitarised Zone

London, Monday—The Nazis' penetration into the demilitarised zone, which alarmed France, has been extended by the occupation of Speyer and Cologne where Nazi troops have taken possession of the Rathaus. The chief burgomaster, Herr Adenaurer, has been suspended by the Nazi Herr Riese.

the beginning of the greatest era of Jewish genocide and persecution, **the Holocaust,** in which over six million Jewish men, women, and children were slaughtered.

The continual stirring up of the nest for almost two thousand years kept the Jewish longing for a return to their ancient homeland alive. In 1897 Theodor Herzl began a new movement for the restoration of the Jewish state which was finally realized in 1948. Some reports indicate that Jews have returned from one hundred twenty nations to Israel, but it is possible that today in Israel Jews may be found from every nation in the world, fulfilling the messianic prophecy that they would come back from **all nations.** This sign is, we believe, the second most important messianic prophetic fulfillment.

▪ ▪ ▪ ▪ ▪

The Jews have returned to Israel from every corner of the world: from China, Singapore, South Africa and Rhodesia, Surinam and New Zealand, Europe, America, and Africa. The return is phenomenal. In 1948 there were six hundred fifty thousand Jews in Israel. The declaration of the state awoke an unbelievable immigration toward Israel when one million Jews came before 1961. They came in two major waves: the first one, the largest in the history of the state, doubled the population in three years. At the time, Jews flocked to Israel from two major centers: the first was from Eastern Europe and the Balkans, and the second, from Asia and Africa. Holocaust survivors came then from Poland, Rumania, and Bulgaria, whereas eastern Jews came from North Africa, Iraq, Yemen, and Turkey. Between 1955 and 1957 came a second wave that counted one hundred sixty-five thousand, mostly from Morocco, but there were considerable numbers from Hungary and the U.S.S.R. Immigration continued, but not until the eighties (when Jews escaped the crumbling Soviet Union) was there a big wave of immigration like in the first three years of the state. In the eighties Israel was a prosperous country and absorbing immigrants was an easier task. The immigration of the fifties is nothing short of a miracle. The state was just beginning to be organized, institutions were barely in existence, and yet enough resources were found to take in a million people—almost twice the number of the population already there.

Operation "Magic Carpet" brought practically the entire Jewish community out of Yemen. It started in December of 1948, following the permission given by Great Britain to open the border of Aden, a British colony in the Arabian peninsula, and allow the Jews to go there from Yemen. In Yemen the obstacles were many. The Imam of Yemen demanded considerable sums of money for permits. In addition, every sultan that controlled some part of the roads demanded a per capita fee for every Jewish person that passed through their territory. Yet the Jews who heard about the declaration of the state and the possibility of going there from Aden walked for weeks to reach Aden, and from there they were flown to Israel.

Operation Ezra and Nehemiah brought the Jews out of Iraq. Jewish agents at that time would go to a country like Iraq. They had to work undercover as they prepared Jews to return by clandestine flights. It was only in 1950 that the Iraqi government agreed to let the Jews go. Once permission was granted, all the Jews were stripped of their Iraqi citizenship and their property was confiscated. The Arab mob conducted numerous terrorist attacks as the Jewish agency was doing its best to get the people out as quickly as possible. Finally in 1951 one hundred fourteen thousand Iraqi Jews were brought to a safe haven in Israel. The Jewish population in Iraq was numerous, Jews having been in Babylon since the exile near-

ly twenty-six hundred years ago. They flourished there until Iraq expelled them following the birth of Israel.

Ethiopian Jews went through similar hardships in the 1980s. Many had to walk across Libya in order to reach secret airplanes in the desert that the U.N. provided. Many died because of the hardships, and some were kidnapped and sold into slavery.

We also have heartwarming stories about Jews who came to Israel out of the Soviet Union. One is particularly well remembered by all Israelis. A plane carrying hundreds of immigrants from Russia couldn't land at the airport because of a scud attack during the Gulf War in 1991. They turned around and landed in Turkey, and then returned the next day.

Today the number of Jews in Israel has increased to approximately five million. This is an unbelievable increase. There are today approximately twelve million Jews in the world, with a large percentage living in the United States (more than three million in New York City alone). But as far as we know, such a thing has never happened before in history—a nation of people being scattered in all the world for two thousand years and still having the desire and motivation to return to the land of their forefathers. This can only be explained as a miracle and the fulfilling of God's plan and purpose for Israel.

—Gilla

▪ ▪ ▪ ▪ ▪

It was in the Babylonian captivity period that the Israelites were first called Jews because they came from the nation of Judah. While most who went into Babylonia were from either the tribes of Judah or Benjamin, there were Israelites from all twelve tribes. There is also a theory (referred to as British Israelism) that during the Assyrian captivity period all the members of the ten northern tribes were killed or went into other nations and became England, America, Denmark, etc. But even after the Assyrian captivity Israelites from all twelve tribes are mentioned in the Bible as being at the Passover in Jerusalem.

During the Babylonian captivity there was some mixing of the tribes, but even after they came back there are references to those Israelites who were members of one of the ten northern tribes. During the period of the Assyrian captivity, many escaped and came back to live in Judea because they could not go back to the northern kingdom. Many of the Israelites of the northern kingdom continue to keep up with their tribal genealogy.

During the Babylonian captivity, because most were from the tribe of Judah, and all were from the nation of Judah, all Israelites began to be called Jews, regardless of their tribal genealogies. Even though we call all Israelites Jews, this does not mean that they are all from the tribe of Judah, although he or she could be.

Sign Number Three

Buying Back the Land

Theodor Herzl had fanned the fires of Zionist nationalism in the late nineteenth century, but the Ottoman Empire was still in control of the Trans-Jordan area. Perhaps with an ulterior motive, Great Britain, in 1903, offered the World Zionist Organization the country of Uganda for the establishing of a new Jewish nation. The appeal was that Uganda in central East Africa was a good land, about twice the land that was included in the old boundaries of Israel, and the Jews could have their own nation immediately. Nevertheless, the World Zionist Organization rejected the offer, citing scriptural reasons that Uganda was not the nation that God promised to the seed of Abraham. One of the scriptures referred to by the World Zionist Organization was a prophecy by Jeremiah:

> Men shall buy fields for money, and subscribe evidences, and seal them, and take witnesses in the land of Benjamin, and in the places about Jerusalem, and in the cities of Judah, and in the cities of the mountains, and in the cities of the valley, and in the cities of the south: for I will cause their captivity to return, saith the LORD.
>
> —Jeremiah 32:44

When the Jews began to return at about the turn of the twentieth century, they first settled in Tel Aviv. There were a few

Jews who already owned homes and properties in other parts of what was then called Palestine, but land and space under their control was limited. So wealthy Jews, supported by outside Zionist contributions, began to buy land from the Turks, Arabs, and others who were willing to sell. The new city on the Mediterranean coast just east of Jaffa was named Tel Aviv, possibly a contemporary spelling for Tel Abib. Abib was the old Hebrew first month of the year, the month of the Passover. It was also the month of Israel's new beginning as they left Egypt. The months were renamed and the calendar changed during the Babylonian captivity. Just as Daniel and his three Hebrew companions were given Babylonian names, so too were the Jewish months.

■ ■ ■ ■ ■

In his book Faith and Fulfillment, *Michael J. Pragai (Valentine, Mitchell & Co., 1985) writes:*

Kibbutz orchard along the Jordan River flowing out of Golan Heights

Modern Tel Aviv as seen from Jaffa

tion the Jewish people clung to life and kept their faith alive. For centuries Christians stood aghast and in wonder, not understanding how this people survived the most wretched and horrible conditions. Sometimes they watched, not in wonder but in puzzlement, in disbelief, and in awe. Perhaps this very wonder in its turn stirred the fires not only of awe, but of hate and envy.

Many solutions were offered and the approach was sometimes theological, sometimes practical, but everyone knew the answer was the return. Christians who knew the prophecies about the return and who were well aware of Jewish hopes and aspirations have often pondered the connection between these biblical prophecies and the Jews living in their midst as outcasts and ever-present targets of hate, discrimination, expulsion, and outright murder. And some have asked: Does Christianity have a task to fulfill while acting in self-fulfillment and promoting salvation and the end of time? Does Christianity have a task to fulfill to ensure that the prophecies of the Jewish return are realized, possibly as a precondition to the fulfillment of the Christian final

> *redemption? Some have asked such questions; others have replied, and over the years many Christian thinkers, theologians, writers, statesmen, and practical politicians have replied in the affirmative: Christians do have a stake in the return. The restoration of the Jewish people to their homeland is part of a Christian understanding of God's promise in the world.*

In 1904 Hayim Weizman, a brilliant young biochemist from Russia (later to be Israel's first president), took a teaching position in Manchester. There he met one such Christian, then the prime minister of Great Britain, Lord Arthur James Balfour (1836–1945). Later he lent his name to the famous Balfour Declaration. Balfour came of a noble Scottish family and was profoundly versed in Old Testament culture and the Hebraic Bible. He liked to read from the prophets, particularly Isaiah. He loved to read aloud, and did so "beautifully and reverently."

In her book Bible and Sword, *Barbara Tuchman quotes from the biography of Lord Balfour, as recorded by his niece Blanche Dougdale:*

> *As he grew, his intellectual admiration and sympathy for certain aspects of Jewish philosophy and culture grew also and the problem of the Jew in the modern world seemed to him of immense importance. He always talked eagerly on this and I remember in childhood imbibing from him the idea that Christian religion and civilization owes to Judaism an immeasurable debt.*

Lt. Col. Patterson, who took command of the Jewish legion in World War I, writes in his book, With the Judeans in the Palestinian Campaign, *published in London in 1922:*

> *Britain's share towards the fulfillment of prophecy must . . . not be forgotten and the names of Mr. Lloyd George and Sir Arthur Balfour, two men who were raised up to deal justly with Israel, will, I feel sure, live in all time in the hearts and affections of the Jewish people. It is owing to the stimulus given by the Balfour Declaration to the soul of Jewry throughout the world that we are now looking upon the wonderful spectacle unfolding itself before our eyes, of the people of Israel returning to the land promised to Abraham and his seed forever.*

Patterson believed that in the future England would be rewarded for the support it gave Israel: "Blessed be he that blesseth thee" (Genesis 27:29). Unfortunately, British politics turned around later because of Arab propaganda and because of the greed for oil.

We mustn't forget Captain Orde Wingate, who trained the Jewish troops in Israel how to fight the Arab gangs. He taught them to fight at night and made them understand that a daring offensive is the best defense. Wingate was Scottish, and his sister Rachel tells us: "It was his mother taught him the biding belief in the Bible. She suckled him on the strong milk of the Old Testament and weaned him on the Psalms and Proverbs." Because of his great sympathy to the Jewish people and his tremendous help in military matters, he was sent away from Palestine. Wingate died in a plane crash in Burma while fighting the Japanese with U.S. troops. His mother-in-law described him to his son after his death:

> *Orde . . . proclaimed his love for Israel and his confidence in the Jewish people . . . all unknowingly with that proclamation of love and confidence Orde assured his immortality. Surely there can be no greater earthly reward: he has become part of the history of Israel.*

And indeed Wingate is known in Israel as "The Friend," and his is a household name in modern Israel.

We should also tell about Walter Clay Lowdermilkr, an eminent American soil conservation expert. He came to Palestine with the great encouragement of his wife Inez, a devout Christian herself. After his visit, Lowdermilkr published a lengthly paper called "Palestine: Land of Promise," in which he proved that in Bible days the population of Israel was more then five million, while in 1939 it was barely one and a half million. He showed how the land could sustain even more than five million people with the proper conservation, forestation, and irrigation. This was a complete rebuff of the British reason for nabbing Jews from Palestine with the argument that the land couldn't sustain so many people.

These are just a few examples of Christians who believed and still believe in the need to help Jewish people get to Israel and who give support for Israel.

—Gilla

▪ ▪ ▪ ▪ ▪

Along with the return of Jews were some misguided Christian groups, even evangelicals, who were going to help Israel bring in the messianic Kingdom. However, the Jews purchased land to develop the *kibbutz* system. The *kibbutzim* were actually Jewish enclaves where the returnees could not only delevop an independent agricultural community, but maintain and expand their cultural influence. The *kibbutz* was actually a communist cell on an enormous scale. This was the way the Jews bought back the land, and gradually refounded a Jewish entity that began to resemble the Old Testament example.

Great Britain gained control and became the protectorate

of Palestine after World War I. The Arabs became alarmed over the continual purchase of land by Jews, and as reported in the January 30, 1936, edition of the *Palestine Post,* the Arab party political leaders petitioned England to:

1. Establish a democratic government in Palestine;
2. Halt Jewish immigration completely; and
3. Make it illegal for any Arab or Palestinian to sell land, buildings, or property to any Jew.

The headline in the same edition of the *Palestine Post* read: **"Land Sales Restrictions Announced by Sir Arthur, High Commissioner."** The British commissioner, giving in to Arab demands, prohibited any further Jewish immigration and placed restrictions on further sales of land to Jews. This was a cruel act by England, as on the same page of the *Palestine Post* was news that Nazi persecution of the Jews had reached genocide proportions. Their escape route to their Jewish homeland had been cut off by Great Britain.

Nevertheless, by this time the population of Tel Aviv had increased to one hundred twenty-five thousand, and the *kibbutz* system was solidly established. The Jews had returned and bought up the land and sealed their deeds. The land was rightfully theirs, and a solid base had been established for a future return of more Jews and the establishing of a Jewish nation. Another prophetic sign of the coming messianic age was being fulfilled.

▪ ▪ ▪ ▪ ▪

The general news media will extrapolate that the buying back of the land by the Jews dispossessed the inhabitants. The population of the land was very sparse at that time, but every piece of land was always purchased. Wealthy Jewish people would

THE PALESTINE POST

Vol. XII No. 2951. JERUSALEM, THURSDAY, JANUARY 30, 1936

Land Sales Restrictions Announced by Sir Arthur

LEGISLATION FOR PROTECTION OF SMALLHOLDERS AND TENANTS

Statement of Arab Party Leaders

An important statement in reply to the Arab demands in a recent memorandum for self-government, stoppage of Jewish immigration and prohibition of land sales to Jews was given by the High Commissioner yesterday morning to representatives of five Arab parties whom His excellency received at the Government Offices.

Concerning the first demand the High Commissioner referred to deputation to the proposals for the establishment of a Legislative Council.

The High Commissioner made it clear that "there could be no question of the total stoppage of Jewish immigration into Palestine." He reaffirmed the principle of absorptive capacity in the admission of immigrants, but added that he intended to keep in close touch with the changing economic situation, for which purpose a statistical bureau had been established.

As regards the third demand for the prohibition of all sales of lands to Jews the High Commissioner, without rejecting the demand, stated that the Secretary of State had approved of legislation preventing land owners from selling any of their land unless he retained a minimum area sufficient for his and his family's subsistence. This legislation would also preclude collusion between buyer and seller by making the minimum area inalienable. The proposed legislation will not apply in the Beersheba district and urban areas, but otherwise it will be of "general application."

The official communique is given below in full and the supplementary explanation which Sir Arthur Wauchope gave to the Arab deputation is summarised. The High Commissioner explained that the Protection of Cultivators Ordinance of 1933 did not assist the small owner or tenant, whose position might be prejudiced, when he has given up his land, by loss of alternative employment, and the natural increase of the population. He stressed that "the process of sale of land by small holders can no longer safely be allowed to go unchecked. He invited the Arab leaders to help in the application of the protective principles of the scheme which "will inevitably occupy a considerable period of time."

The Arab leaders prsent at the interview yesterday were Jamaal Effendi el Husseini, representing the Palestine Arab Party; Ragheb Bey Nashashibi, National Defence Party; Ishac Effendi Budeiri, Reform Party; Abdul Latif Bey Salah, National Bloc; and Yacoub Effendi Ghussein, the Youth Organization.

The **Palestine Post** understands that Jamal Eff Husseini acted as spokesman during this interview which included a free discussion lasting an hour.

To Jamal Effendi's assertion that the Government's action left things much as they were, the High Commissioner is understood to have replied in the negative, pointing out that the Legislative Council was designed gradually to lead to self-government.

Official Communique

It will be recalled that at the end of November the leaders of the Arab political parties submitted as memorandum to the High Commissioner setting out their main demands, namely:

(a) that a democratic government should be established in Palestine;
(b) that Jewish immigration should cease completely;
(c) that all sales of land to Jews should be prohibited.

That memorandum was transmitted by His Excellency the High Commissioner to the Secretary of State who, having given it very careful consideration, communicated to His Excellency by telegraph the following reply:—

Elective Legislative

(a) the demand for the establishment of a democratic Government has been answered by the

(Continued on Page Five)

come to Palestine and buy up the available land. A good example of this would be the Rothschild family. Jews who would wanted to come to Israel soon after 1900 would turn to the Rothschilds for funds to buy up the land. The land had to be, for the most part, purchased from the Ottoman Empire. Sometimes the Jews would have to buy the land twice, because they would buy it from an Arab that did not have clear title. But even though a piece of land had to be bought a second time, a full price was always paid. Also, only after the land had been legally purchased would the Jews begin living on it and farming it.

Jeremiah demonstrates his faith in the return to the land of Israel by personally redeeming a family-owned field and paying its full value. This is recounted in chapter thirty-two just before the verses Rev. Hutchings cited in relation to the Zionist Congress. In the beginning of the chapter Jeremiah actively shows his total faith in the return of Israel. The circumstance is striking. He is in jail because he foretold the Babylonian exile, yet he knows full well that his descendants will be back to Israel.

> *So Hanameel mine uncle's son came to me in the court of the prison according to the word of the LORD, and said unto me, Buy my field, I pray thee, that is in Anathoth, which is in the country of Benjamin: for the right of inheritance is thine, and the redemption is thine; buy it for thyself. Then I knew that this was the word of the LORD. And I bought the field of Hanameel my uncle's son, that was in Anathoth, and weighed him the money, even seventeen shekels of silver.*
>
> *—Jeremiah 32:8–9*

After the Babylonian captivity Cyrus gave the land and Jerusalem back to the returning Israelites, so the buying back of the land that was prophesied by Jeremiah doubtless refers to our times and indicates another fulfillment of a messianic promise. This might be construed as a partial fulfillment, as the Arabs still own much of the land of Israel.

—Gilla

Sign Number Four

Israel Reborn in a Day

One of the most impressive messianic signs is the refounding of Israel as a nation on May 14, 1948.

We note again that the main concern of the prophets of Israel was the arrival of the messianic age in which all the covenants God made with the fathers would be honored and every promise to the nation fulfilled. The prophet Isaiah arrived at the grand finale in the last chapter of his book of prophecy: "For, behold, the LORD will come with fire, and with his chariots like a whirlwind, to render his anger with fury, and his rebuke with flames of fire" (Isaiah 66:15).

A day of Shabbat at the Western Wall

Basic Jewish and Christian eschatology agree in the manner the Messiah will appear and what will follow in the wake of His coming. The difference is that the vast majority of the Jews from the time of Jesus to the present have never accepted Him as the promised Messiah. Observing Jews look for the coming Messiah; Christians look for Jesus Christ the Messiah to come again. In any event, from a Jewish perspective the nation must be refounded before the Messiah would come; from a Christian position the nation of Israel must be refounded before Jesus Christ will bodily return to this earth. Jesus Christ in the Olivet Discourse describes His return in much the same manner as Isaiah describes the Messiah's coming, which also coincides with the coming of the King of Kings as foretold by the apostle John in Revelation chapter nineteen.

Before the coming of the Lord to put down all enemies and establish His Kingdom, Isaiah referred to a preceding event that would happen:

> Before she travailed, she brought forth; before her pain came, she was delivered of a man child. Who hath heard such a thing? who hath seen such things? Shall the earth be made to bring forth in one day? or shall a nation be born at once? for as soon as Zion travailed, she brought forth her children. Shall I bring to the birth, and not cause to bring forth? saith the LORD: shall I cause to bring forth, and shut the womb? saith thy God.
>
> —Isaiah 66:7–9

Christian theologians present the explanation that the man-child which Israel brought forth before there were any birth-pangs was Jesus Christ. There was no travail in birth because Israel never recognized Him. However, the prophet continued to describe Israel's travail in the birth of the nation that would be born in a day. This event, according to the context of the prophecy, would occur before the Lord's coming. We believe this prophecy had a fulfillment on May 14, 1948.

The headline of the *Palestine Post* of May 16, 1948, read: **"State of Israel Is Born."** The newspaper account read in part:

> The first independent Jewish state in nineteen centuries was born in Tel Aviv as the British Mandate over Palestine came to an end at midnight on Friday, and it was immediately subjected to the test of fire. As the State of Israel was proclaimed, the battle for Jerusalem raged, with most of the city falling to the Jews. At the same time, President Truman announced that the United States would accord recognition of the new State. A few hours later, Palestine was invaded by Moslem armies from the south, east, and north.

General George Marshall, spokesman for the U.S. State Department, had wired the premier of the new state of Israel, David Ben Gurion, that if he declared an independent state, that five Arab armies would immediately march against the new nation and within three days there would not be a Jew left alive in Palestine. However, the prophet Isaiah twenty-seven hundred years before had prophesied that God would not allow this to happen. He wrote: "Shall I bring to the birth, and not cause to bring forth? saith the Lord: shall I cause to bring forth, and shut the womb? saith thy God." The prophet also promised, ". . . as soon as Zion travailed, she brought forth her children." General Marshall was wrong because he had not read Isaiah chapter sixty-six. A ragtag Jewish army with few arms and little training defeated five well-trained and fully equipped armies with artillery, planes, and tanks

If you can't come to town, please telephone 4607
Lighting, Heating, Cooking, Refrigeration
CARL MARX
3 PRINCESS MARY AVE., JERUSALEM

JERUSALEM
SUNDAY, MAY 16, 1948

THE PALESTINE POST

PRICE: 25 MILS
VOL. XXIII. No. 6714

THE PALESTINE POST
THE SUBSCRIPTION DEPARTMENT has returned to The Palestine Post offices, Hassolel Street, Jerusalem, Tel. 4233.

STATE OF ISRAEL IS BORN

The first independent Jewish State in 19 centuries was born in Tel Aviv as the British Mandate over Palestine came to an end at midnight on Friday, and it was immediately subjected to the test of fire. As "Medinat Yisrael" (State of Israel) was proclaimed, the battle for Jerusalem raged, with most of the city falling to the Jews. At the same time, President Truman announced that the United States would accord recognition to the new State. A few hours later, Palestine was invaded by Moslem armies from the south, east and north, and Tel Aviv was raided from the air. On Friday the United Nations Special Assembly adjourned after adopting a resolution to appoint a mediator but without taking any action on the Partition Resolution of November 29.

Yesterday the battle for the Jerusalem-Tel Aviv road was still under way, and two Arab villages were taken. In the north, Acre town was captured, and the Jewish Army consolidated its positions in Western Galilee.

Most Crowded Hours in Palestine's History

JEWS TAKE OVER SECURITY ZONES

Egyptian Air Force Spitfires Bomb Tel Aviv; One Shot Down

U.S. RECOGNIZES JEWISH STATE

Proclamation by Head Of Government

David Ben Gurion, Prime Minister

2 Columns Cross Southern Border

Etzion Settlers Taken P.O.W.

Special Assembly Adjourns

A Good Thing

EMERGENCY

War Office Says Legion Had Left

2 Villages Taken In Road Battle

EGYPTIAN INVASION BEFORE U.N. SECURITY COUNCIL

GROMYKO TO BE REPLACED

Sir Alan Sails From Palestine

ACRE CAPTURED

Double Summer Time in Jerusalem

The Palestine Post

Front page of Palestine Post from May 16, 1948

from five Arab nations. As prophesied, Jews from all nations afterward began to return. Nothing like this had ever happened before. After being scattered into all nations for over nineteen centuries, a remnant returns and immediately becomes a nation.

■ ■ ■ ■ ■ ■

The state of Israel greatly owes its birth to one man, David Ben Gurion. Born in Poland in 1886, Ben Gurion came to Palestine at the age of twenty. He gradually became the unquestioned leader of the Labor Party and of the Zionist Organization. He centralized power and controlled everything. Nowadays he would be considered a dictator, and Israel's democracy wouldn't suffer this kind of control, but Ben Gurion was the man chosen by God to further God's plan for Israel. In spite of very strong opposition within the Hagana (the military organization of the Labor Party) and inside the Zionist Organization, he made the decision that May 14, 1948, was the right time. He came to the conclusion that in order to draw Jewish people and receive help from other nations, Israel must be an independent state. In spite of the opposition and although he knew full well that the Arabs would not accept the new state and Israel would immediately be faced with a terrible war, he proceeded with his plan. Ben Gurion seemed to have a God-sent message that the time for Israel to be reborn was at hand. This was Ben Gurion's mission in life.

When I lead tour groups by the kibbutz *that Ben Gurion established in the Negev Desert, we stop at the small museum maintained in his memory. But the truly impressive part is a stop at the gravesites where he and his wife were buried. It is a very lovely spot and a very meaningful one. The graves overlook the wilderness of Zin through which the children of Israel came into the Promised Land. Ben Gurion firmly believed that every Jewish person should live in Israel. How appropriate that he should be buried at the road of entry to Israel. Thousands of people who come to the gravesite look at the road of the Exodus and remember Ben Gurion's message.*

—Gilla

Who Holds the Reins? Page Three

THE PALESTINE POST

JERUSALEM
THURSDAY, JAN. 30, 1936.

PRICE: TEN MILS
VOL. XII. 2951.

Land Sales Restrictions Announced by Sir Arthur

LEGISLATION FOR PROTECTION OF SMALLHOLDERS AND TENANTS

Statement to Arab Party Leaders

16 Pages

The Negus Returns Home PAGE SEVEN

THE PALESTINE POST

JERUSALEM
FRIDAY, MAY 8, 1936

VOL. XII. 3035.
PRICE: TEN MILS

Arabs Decide on Civil Disobedience

REFUSAL TO PAY TAXES AFTER MAY 15

THE PALESTINE POST

FRIDAY NOVEMBER 11 1938 JERUSALEM

NAZI HOOLIGANS VENT WRATH ON THE JEWS THROUGHOUT GERMANY

LATE Edition

THE PALESTINE POST

JERUSALEM
WEDNESDAY, May 31, 1944

PRICE: 15 MILS
VOL. XIX. Number 5500

GREAT POWERS TO POLICE WORLD

HULL ON U.S. PEACE PLANS

Sign Number Five

The Order of the Return

As also referred to, the second most important messianic sign in Israel has been the return of Jews from all the nations of the world where they have been scattered. Egypt in the Bible is given as an example of the world, or a type of world, and God demonstrated His will and His power in bringing the children of Israel to the Promised Land. God is once more demonstrating His will and His power in bringing them out of the world back into the land He gave them. In addition, not only is God bringing them back as prophesied, even more miraculous the prophet Isaiah foretold the exact order of their return.

> For I am the Lord thy God, the Holy One of Israel, thy Saviour: I gave Egypt for thy ransom, Ethiopia and Seba for thee. Since thou wast precious in my sight, thou hast been honourable, and I have loved thee: therefore will I give men for thee, and people for thy life. Fear not: for I am with thee: I will bring thy seed from the [1] east, and gather thee from the [2] west; I will say to the [3] north, Give up; and to the [4] south, Keep not back: bring my sons from far, and my daughters from the ends of the earth; . . . Ye are my witnesses, saith the Lord, and my servant whom I have chosen: that ye may know and believe me, and understand that I am he: before me there was no God formed, neither

European Jews, Chinese Jews, and Ethiopian Jews returning to Israel from 1950s to 1980s.

> shall there be after me. . . . This people have I formed for myself; they shall shew forth my praise. But thou hast not called upon me, O Jacob; but thou hast been weary of me, O Israel.
>
> —Isaiah 43:3–6, 10, 21–22

Isaiah prophesied that though Israel would not believe, when the time for the Messiah was at hand, the Lord would regather them in their unbelief. Israel would first return from the east, and according to the *Judaic Encyclopedia,* in 1900 there were three hundred thousand Jews in Turkey; in 1939, there were only thirty thousand. The same percentages of Jewish immigration to Israel also applied to Jordan, Syria, Iraq, Yemen, and other nations in the Middle East.

The second stage of Jewish immigration came from the west, the nations of Europe. In 1939 the Jewish population of Europe was nine million, four hundred eight thousand; in 1948, it had dropped to three million, seven hundred eight thousand. After the Nazi Holocaust in which almost six million Jews were killed, additional thousands fled to Israel seeking a place of peace and safety.

The third phase of Jewish immigration, according to prophecy, was to come from the north. Until the *glasnost* policies of Gorbachev were initiated in Russia in 1988, the Jews were not allowed to emigrate. Then, a few began to return through Helsinki; but the prime minister of Finland closed the exit door because of Arab pressure. A constituent of our ministry, Siiki, and a friend of the prime minister's wife, informed him that unless he opened the door to Jewish emigration from Russia again, God would do to him what He did to the king of Edom. To date, over four hundred thousand Russian Jews have gone to Israel.

The fourth and final phase of the return of a remnant to prepare for the coming of Messiah would be from the south, according to Isaiah. In 1991 approximately fourteen thousand black Jews (Falasha) were flown out of Ethiopia to Israel in Operation Solomon. According to tradition, the black Jews of Ethiopia are descendants of a son born to the Queen of Sheba by Solomon (1 Kings 10). Thus, the order of the return of a Jewish remnant to await Messiah's appearance is exactly as prophesied.

Matthew 8:11 clearly is a reference to Gentile participation in the Kingdom of Heaven, the messianic age. In this scripture Jesus mentioned only two directions, the east and the west. Luke 13:29 indicates a separation or a difference between saved Jews and unsaved Jews. Here it would seem that Jesus is referring to regathering of those Jews acceptable for the Kingdom age, and in this scripture all four directions are mentioned in the same order given by Isaiah: east, west, north, and south.

■ ■ ■ ■ ■

Liberated Jews after Holocaust as they are dispersed to various countries

The order as given in Isaiah's prophecy is indeed amazing. There were more than three million Jews left in Russia after 1948. The Soviet Union would not allow them to re-

turn. However, today there are more than one million who have immigrated to Israel from Russia. The number of Ethiopian Jews who have returned is near twenty thousand. This was an unbelievable operation. It happened right after the Gulf War in 1991. They were brought secretly to Addis Ababa. The government officials were bribed with millions of dollars to close their eyes and not say anything about Israeli agents who were in Ethiopia to successfully complete this operation. The planes were packed. The Ethiopian Jews were very poor and thin, some weighing no more than eighty pounds. An average 747 would normally carry about four hundred passengers, but with the light Ethiopian Jews the pilots could get from twelve to fifteen hundred in one plane. After landing in Israel, they were taken to hotels, to the kibbutz, *waiting or holding centers, and the Israeli people came forth and brought food and clothing. All Israel rejoiced that another part of the regathering of the people had been completed and the children of Zion had come back to the Promised Land. The air force pilots, some veterans of many wars, remember this as their most beautiful hour.*

—Gilla

Operation Solomon: the return of Ethiopian Jews to Israel

Sign Number Six

A Pure Language

According to the Bible, before the Tower of Babel incident, which occurred approximately forty-three hundred years ago by Ussher's calculations, there was only one language used in oral communications. If there was a method of written communications, it would appear to have been based upon pictorial symbols much like ancient Egyptian, Chinese, and other Oriental and Semitic writings. The multiplicity of languages, again according to Scripture, occurred suddenly. It is thought by some that perhaps the language spoken by Adam was Hebrew. We know that Adam and Eve had conversations and that Adam also answered the Lord. This language that Adam spoke must have been passed on to succeeding generations until after the Flood. But whether it was Hebrew that the pre-Babel peoples spoke cannot be proven as far as we know, although this is a pleasant thought.

English is at best a three-dimensional language—the subject, the message, and the situation. Hebrew is a four-dimensional language. In studying the Hebrew biblical text, the reader not only receives knowledge of the subject, the message, and the situation, but also received is the flavor, aroma, the feeling, or mental environment in which the words were written. In other words, a mental perception or image is given that is absent from English. As Suzanne Haïk-Vantoura states on page 369 of her book, *The Music of the Bible:* "In the Hebrew text of the psalms the words are simplistic, yet in unison they burst forth like blossoming flowers." Gail Riplinger, in her book *The Language of the King James Bible,* in great detail shows how that in subsequent translations words have lost their pictorial meanings. Therefore, in the newer translations, instead of three-dimensional English, we have only two-dimensional English. Just because the scholars who worked on the Tyndale, Geneva, and later the King James Bible, lived four to five hundred years ago does not mean they were less qualified to translate Hebrew and Greek into English. In fact, these men were far superior to modern translators. Most of those who worked on the King James Version knew three languages, and some knew seven or eight languages. In our opinion, each newer version of the Bible is a further deprecation of the original inspired text.

Even at the time of Jesus the Hebrew spoken and written by Isaiah had been corrupted by Babylonian, Assyrian, Greek, Latin, and Aramaic. The sign over Jesus' head when He was crucified had to be written in Hebrew, Greek, and Latin, so

Many reliefs of the Hebrew pure language are found throughout Israel

that everyone would understand (Luke 23:38).

After A.D. 70 when the majority of Jews in Israel were scattered into all nations during the Diaspora, they learned or adopted the language of the country in which they lived. While many Jews over the centuries continued to speak their national language, the Hebrew gradually became even more corrupted. At the turn of the twentieth century, as more and more Jews began to migrate back to Israel, there was a problem in that they could not communicate. They either spoke different languages, or a Hebrew dialect that was not readily or commonly understood. In 1928 a Jew by the name of Eliezer Ben Yehuda, evidently with the backing of the Zionist Organization, got Hebrew recognized as the official language of the return. This was also foretold as a messianic sign in Zephaniah 3:8–10:

> Therefore wait ye upon me, saith the LORD, until the day that I rise up to the prey: for my determination is to gather the nations, that I may assemble the kingdoms, to pour upon them mine indignation, even all my fierce anger: for all the earth shall be devoured with the fire of my jealousy. For then will I turn to the people a pure language, that they may all call upon the name of the LORD, to serve him with one consent. From beyond the rivers of Ethiopia my suppliants, even the daughter of my dispersed, shall bring mine offering.

This prophecy definitely has a latter-day setting when the Jews began returning from all nations. The time is given prior to the battle of Armageddon. The prophet indicated that even the Jews who return from Ethiopia, or beyond Ethiopia, will have to learn Hebrew. The black Jews from Ethiopia today in Israel speak Hebrew like everyone else.

▪ ▪ ▪ ▪ ▪ ▪

Hebrew is the vernacular language of Israel. Hebrew is an important and essential identification of the nation of Israel. Israel is identified as a peculiar nation by first, a race of people who descended from Abraham through Isaac and Jacob; secondly, Israel is identified by territory, the boundaries of a piece of land in the Middle East; thirdly, by a language, Hebrew, the language spoken by the patriarchs and the prophets; fourth, by an adherence and practice of faith in the Mosaic Law and the Word of the Lord as committed to the prophets; and fifth, in a holy place designated the Temple Mount on Mount Moriah. If any part of the total identification is missing, then the nation of Israel is not complete.

It is indeed a remarkable fulfillment of messianic signs that the Ethiopian Jews have returned, and like all Israeli citizens, they had to learn to speak Hebrew. Hebrew is the language of the Knesset; the language of the news media; the language used in our schools; and the language of business. In Israel we do not have a controversy over whether English, French, Spanish, Russian, or any language other than Hebrew is our national language.

However, we are indeed fortunate that in Jews returning from all nations, the tourist or visitor to Israel can find Israelis who can speak almost any known language. We have national tourist guides who can speak French, Spanish, English, etc. But as a nation we are proud of our Hebrew language. It is the language of our people and the language that God chose to give us in the Old Testament.

—Gilla

Sign Number Seven

The Shekel

We read in Genesis 2 that God made gold and it was good. Gold was established as the basis for all money. Later in Genesis chapter twenty-three we read about silver as also being a metal of exchange, but not nearly as valuable as gold. Even later in the Bible we read that paper notes were written to be redeemable in gold or silver, but sometimes the paper promises to pay were no good. Every paper currency in history to this date has, sooner or later, depreciated in value or become totally worthless. Although gold or silver may vary in value according to weight, these metals remain the only stable units of exchange in the world.

The first Hebrew unit of monetary exchange, the shekel, is first mentioned in Genesis 23:15. Abraham bought a burial site for Sarah at a cost of four hundred shekels. A shekel is approximately one-third of an ounce of silver, or approximately two dollars at the current rate of exchange in 1999. Today, the land would be worth approximately eight hundred dollars. A talent is three thousand shekels of silver. It is thought that the first silver or gold coins to appear were in Assyria at about 900 B.C. It is possible that a shekel could have been either a minted coin predating the Assyrian coins, or it could have been a silver nugget of about one-third of an ounce.

We read in Exodus 30:11–16, that every Israelite male of the age of twenty years or older had to make an offering of

Coins of Israel

one-half shekel to maintain services in the Tabernacle. However, according to Ezekiel 45:12, the offering to the Temple required by each Israelite could run as high as sixty shekels of silver. When Israel became a nation in 1948, there was no national currency. The British pound or the U.S. dollar were the most common monies used for exchange units. Finally in 1980 the Knesset restored the shekel as the official unit of exchange in Israel. We read from Ezekiel 45:12–13, 16: "And the shekel [shall be] twenty gerahs. . . . This is the oblation that ye shall offer. . . . All the people of the land shall give this oblation for the prince in Israel."

The restoration of the shekel was an important messianic sign because, according to Ezekiel, when the Messiah appears offerings and oblations must be made in shekels. When we go to Israel today, we convert our dollars into shekels and make our purchases in the traditional Old Testament currency.

■ ■ ■ ■ ■ ■

When the state of Israel was refounded, it was still under the influence of the British Mandate. From 1918 to 1948 the British government ran the government of Israel, which at that time was called Palestine. The money used was the Palestine pound, which was related to the English pound. For many years after Israel again became a nation, the pound remained the money used by the people.

I remember when I was a child there was also the lyra, which is Arabic for the British pound. In 1980 the government went back to the shekel, the money that dated back to the time the Jews returned from the Babylonian captivity.

The design on the coins is that of ancient coins uncovered in excavations. The one shekel coin is a lily like the oldest coin dating from 600 B.C. uncovered in a dig. The inscription on it said Judea, referring to the Persian promise in that time. The same graphics are imprinted on the new shekel.

The shekel is now the official monetary unit once more, but unfortunately we still have a problem with inflation, and the shekel is continuing to be devalued. The shekel is now worth about twenty-five cents, or one-fourth of a dollar.

—Gilla

THE PALESTINE POST

JERUSALEM
Wednesday, May 2, 1945

PRICE: 15 MILS
VOL. XX, No. 5781

HITLER'S DEATH ANNOUNCED

DOENITZ SUCCEEDS FUEHRER; SAYS GERMANS WILL FIGHT ON

THE PALESTINE POST

JERUSALEM
SUNDAY, DEC. 16, 1945

NAZIS ADMIT MURDERING 6 MILLION JEWS IN EUROPE

NOT ENOUGH TO SATISFY HIMMLER

THE PALESTINE POST

JERUSALEM
Tuesday, February 19, 1946

PRICE 15 MILS
VOL. XXI., No. 6029

NO PLACE FOUND FOR JEWS IN EUROPE

"D.P. CAMPS MUST BE CLEARED"

THE PALESTINE POST

JERUSALEM
TUESDAY, JULY 23, 1946

PRICE 15 MILS
VOL. XXI. No. 6156

41 DEAD, 53 INJURED, 52 MISSING, IN TERRORIST ATTACK ON SECRETARIAT

NOON-HOUR OUTRAGE BY GANG; BOMBS IN MILK CANS; SIR JOHN SHAW AND SOME SENIOR OFFICERS SAFE

At least 41 men and women were killed, 53 were injured, and another 52 were still reported missing at midnight, as a result of a terrorist attack shortly after noon yesterday which destroyed a large section of the offices of the Secretariat of the Palestine Government housed in the south-west corner of the King David Hotel.

Senior and Junior Civil Servants — British, Jewish, and Arab — are among the dead. Of those identified, the names of 23 Palestinians were released for publication, but the identity of five British officials and seven Army and Police personnel will not be disclosed until tonight, after their next-of-kin have been notified.

THE PALESTINE POST

JERUSALEM
TUESDAY, AUGUST 13, 1946

PRICE: 15 MILS
VOL. XXI. NO. 6175

REFUGEES NOT TO BE LANDED IN PALESTINE

LONDON ORDERS ILLEGAL IMMIGRANTS TO BE SENT TO "CYPRUS OR ELSEWHERE" PENDING DECISION ON THEIR FUTURE

Sign Number Eight

Cities of Israel

The thirty-eighth and thirty-ninth chapters of Ezekiel describe an invasion of Israel by an alliance of Arab armies under the leadership of a nation from the north called "Gog." Many scholars believe that "Gog" refers to Russia in the last days. It appears that according to Ezekiel's prophecy, this invasion is to come after a peace arrangement has been made. Of course, since 1948 when Israel was refounded as a nation, there have been three major invasions of Israel and many lesser efforts. All have been unsuccessful so far, and according to Ezekiel the invasion mentioned in chapters thirty-eight and thirty-nine of his prophecy will suffer an even greater defeat than previous ones.

The thirty-sixth and thirty-seventh chapters of Ezekiel appear to refer to the period of the return up to the Tribulation, or the "time of Jacob's trouble." We read about some of the specifics of the return and the resettlement of the Promised Land in Ezekiel 36:11, 24:

> And I will multiply upon you man and beast; and they shall increase and bring fruit: and I will settle you after your old estates, and will do better unto you than at your beginnings: . . . For I will take you from among the heathen, and gather you out of all countries, and will bring you into your own land.

We read also this latter-day promise in Isaiah 44:26: "... Thou shalt be inhabited; and to the cities of Judah, Ye shall be built, and I will raise up the decayed places thereof."

We associated the cities of Israel with their biblical names. However, we have to remember that after A.D. 70 the Romans were in control of the cities, and many were given Roman names; then the Moslems came in and renamed some of the cities with Moslem or Arab names; then the Crusaders were in the land for two hundred years; then the Byzantines and the Turks. During the Byzantine period, cities in the land would be given names like Reshat, Fahma, Seilum, Amud, etc. But the promise to Israel was that when the Lord gathered them back into the land, the cities would be named and settled according to their old biblical names and in the same location.

In going through Israel today, the tourist will find that Nazareth is Nazareth, Cana is Cana, Be'ersheva is Be'ersheva, Elath is Elath, and even the little village of Nain is called Nain today. Almost without exception the cities have been renamed with their biblical names and settled in the same places as they were in Bible times. This is indeed another remarkable messianic sign today in Israel.

One of the possible exceptions, however, would be the city of Bethany on the east side of the Mount of Olives, which is still an Arab city. It was in Bethany that Jesus said, "The poor ye have with you always."

Beersheva, Israel

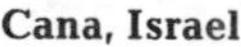

Cana, Israel

Nazareth, Israel

▪ ▪ ▪ ▪ ▪ ▪

The Palestinians who live in the old city of Bethany do call it by another name. However, the name of Lazarus has been preserved. Bethany means "the house of poverty," and even this might be considered a messianic sign because Bethany is still a very poor city. And although the Palestinians call their city by another name, Israelis, Americans, and most other tourists still refer to it as Bethany.

Generally speaking, names of places in Israel are always the old biblical or historical names. Many names were kept by the Arabs, or at least the same root of the name. Carmel became Carmil. Deborah became Dabburiya. One amusing name is Offra. There were several Offra's in biblical days, like the town of Gideon in the Jezreel Valley. In Arabic, the word offra *means "devil." The people were afraid of the name, so they renamed it Taybe, which means "good." We know, therefore, that the Arabic villages called Taybe were all called Offra in Bible days.*

—Gilla

1948

MAY

Su	Mo	Tu	We	Th	Fr	Sa
						1
2	3	4	5	6	7	8
9	10	11	12	13	14	15
16	17	18	19	20	21	22
23	24	25	26	27	28	29
30	31					

1. Korea: Soviet-supported govt. in North adopts constitution claiming sovereignty over whole country (→ 10).

1. N.Y.: Jewish Agency demands U.N. action, as Syrian army invades Palestine (→ 14).

3. U.S. Supreme Court bans pacts barring Negroes from owning real estate (→ 7/17).

3. U.S.: Pulitzers go to Tennessee Williams for "A Streetcar Named Desire," and Michener for "Tales of the South Pacific."

4. Athens: 24 leftists executed for murder (→ 16).

9. Socialists name Norman Thomas for president (→ 6/25).

10. Korea: Six mil. go to polls in South, vote in rightists (→ 31).

13. U.S.: ERP bars aid to nations giving military aid to U.S.S.R. (→ 10/6/49).

14. Tel Aviv: State of Israel proclaimed (→ 15).

15. Egypt invades Israel, bombs Tel Aviv (→ 16).

16. Tel Aviv: Chaim Weizmann named Israeli president, as troops of five Arab nations advance in Israel (→ 20).

17. Moscow: Stalin praises presidential platform of Truman foe Henry Wallace (→ 6/25).

17. Soviet censures Tito for rebuke of Cominform (→ 6/28).

19. Congress passes Mundt-Nixon Bill, requiring Communists to register with govt. (→ 29).

20. N.Y.: U.N. Council names Count Folke Bernadotte U.N. mediator for Palestine (→ 22).

22. British down four Egyptian Spitfires over Palestine (→ 31).

24. Helsinki: Communists strike to protest dismissal of Interior Min. Yrjoe Leino (→ 8/18/49).

29. Washington: Wallace blasts Mundt-Nixon Bill as Cold War act against U.S.S.R. (→ 6/2).

31. Seoul: Syngman Rhee claims rule for all Korea (→ 8/12).

DEATHS

2. Wilhelm von Opel, German auto pioneer.

23. Claude McKay, black American Marxist poet (*9/15/1890).

State of Israel comes into existence

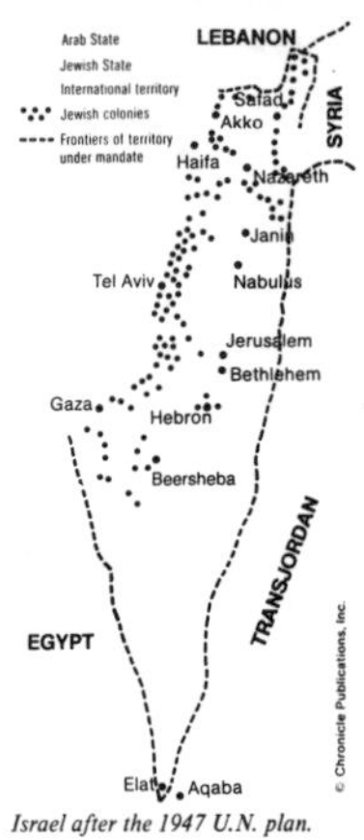

Israel after the 1947 U.N. plan.

Israel after independence.

May 31. The new state of Israel, which is just two weeks old, is under siege and shrinking. It is under attack from the north, east and south by enemies intent upon forcing it into extinction. The Arab League has rejected an appeal from the United Nations for a cease-fire.

The fighting started as soon as the British mandate expired on the 15th and Israel came into existence. Troops from Syria and Lebanon attacked in the north. Forces from Transjordan and Iraq moved in from the east. And Egypt invaded from the south.

An Israeli spokesman says the country is ready to respect a cease-fire, "but we have no intention of accepting the condition, suggested in most Arab public statements, that we should abandon the Jewish state. That would be paramount to political surrender." The Arab states, for their part, refuse to even negotiate with Israel.

The military pressures on Israel are formidable. Iraq says it has cut the coastal road from the capital of Tel Aviv to Haifa. And Transjordan forces say they have defeated an Israeli effort to open the highway between Tel Aviv and Jerusalem. Tel Aviv has been bombarded from the air for two weeks.

The American Consul General, Thomas Wasson, was shot to death by a sniper in Jerusalem last week. Wasson was wounded while returning from the French Consulate, where he had been trying to arrange a truce in the fighting. A spokesman for the Haganah, the Israeli army, says Wasson was killed by an Arab sniper.

The United States, an early supporter of Israel, unexpectedly gave diplomatic recognition to the country on the 15th. Emotions and sentiment in favor of Israel run high in parts of America. In New York, tens of thousands of people were turned away when a "Salute to Israel" rally packed Madison Square Garden. The meeting was sponsored by the American Zionist Emergency Council. Many of the speakers appealed for a lifting of the arms embargo on Israel.

This enthusiasm for Israel is not matched in Britain. After withdrawing its last High Commissioner from Palestine, the government in London refused to establish relations with Tel Aviv. "There is no need to hurry," one British official said. Britain has also made no effort to stop the Arab armies which have invaded Israel. And some British diplomats are going so far as to doubt whether the Arab invasion is an act of aggression.

The hostilities in Israel have not stopped Jews from around the world from applying for immigration to Israel. Hundreds of Jews have already arrived from France and Cyprus, where they had been interned by the British.

One of the first actions of the new Israeli government was to open its doors to all Jews. A proclamation invited Jews to join "the struggle for the fulfillment of the dream of generations, the redemption of Israel."

Prime Minister Ben Gurion read the proclamation as the Israeli flag, the Star of David, flew over his head. Dr. Chaim Weizmann was elected provisional President (→ 6/1).

Weizmann, Israel's first President.

Composition of the population of Palestine from 1922 to 1947

	Arabs	Jews	Percentage of Jews among the total population
1922	668,258	83,790	11.1%
1931	858,708	174,606	16.9%
1936	982,614	384,078	28.1%
1939	1,056,241	445,457	29.7%
1945	1,255,708	554,329	30.6%
1947	1,319,434	589,341	30.9%

Sign Number Nine

Cities of Exception

In discussing the messianic promise that the cities of Israel would be settled and renamed after their old estates, we concluded that this had been done as the Jews began to return to their land at the turn of the twentieth century. However, Jesus said that there would be three cities in Israel that would never be inhabited again. This prophecy is found in Matthew 11:20–21, 23:

> Then began he to upbraid the cities wherein most of his mighty works were done, because they repented not: Woe unto thee, Chorazin! woe unto thee, Bethsaida! for if the mighty works, which were done in you, had been done in Tyre and Sidon, they would have repented long ago in sackcloth and ashes. . . . And thou, Capernaum, which art exalted unto heaven, shalt be brought down to hell: for if the mighty works, which have been done in thee, had been done in Sodom, it would have remained until this day.

We read in Matthew 9:1 that Capernaum was Jesus' "own city." After Jesus was rejected at Nazareth and the men of that city tried to kill Him, He went to Capernaum. Jesus indicated that Capernaum was a large and prosperous city—that it was exalted to heaven. The city was on the main road from Jerusalem that went along the northern shore of the Sea of

Synagogue ruins in Capernaum, Israel

Galilee and continued to Damascus. The Romans had a tariff station at Capernaum and Matthew was a tax collector. But it was here that Jesus had relatives, and it was here that He called His apostles.

Jesus did not have a home in Capernaum, or even a house to live in. He said that He did not even have His own place to lay His head. The scriptures indicate that most of the time He must have lived with Peter's family. Although Peter was hot tempered and impetuous, he must have been a good husband, because he suffered his mother-in-law to live with him. Paul also indicated that when Peter went abroad he took his wife with him. It was in this area that Jesus gave the Sermon on the Mount, calmed the waves of the sea, divided the loaves and fishes to feed thousands, and so many came to Him to be healed at Peter's house that the sick and lame were let down through the roof. The foundation of Peter's house is still in evidence today.

The good news, according to John the Baptist, was "repent, for the kingdom of heaven is at hand." This was also the gospel of the Kingdom that Jesus declared. But even though the people of Capernaum witnessed Jesus' miracles, heard His message, and saw the hundreds that He healed, they did not repent. They did not accept Him as the Messiah. So Jesus said that if He had done the same miracles in Sodom, even that wicked and evil city would have repented, and so He pronounced a curse upon the city. Capernaum is one of the biblical cities in Israel that has not been rebuilt or resettled. It is still in ruins.

Another city that Jesus cursed was Bethsaida. From the biblical description, it appears that Bethsaida was located at the northeast corner of the Sea of Galilee where the Jordan empties into the sea, and near the land of the Gadarenes, which is on the east side. Peter evidently lived in Bethsaida before he moved to Capernaum. Bethsaida was also the home of Philip and Andrew, and it was here that Jesus walked on the water to the boat carrying the disciples. This miracle is recorded in Mark 6:48. Jesus did other miracles and presented messianic signs to the inhabitants of Bethsaida, but like

Carved menorah on column from synagogue ruins in Capernaum

those at Capernaum, they neither repented nor received Him as the promised Messiah. There are only a few blocks of masonry sticking out of the ground that marks the site of Bethsaida. It has, as Jesus prophesied, not been rebuilt.

Another city that Jesus cursed was Chorazin. Chorazin was located approximately five miles north of Capernaum on top of a mountain. The Bible mentions no one of importance as coming from this city, nor is there any record of Jesus even visiting Chorazin. We know that it was a fairly large town for that time. It had a large and well built synagogue, as well as many other buildings. However, Jesus or some of the apostles and disciples must have given a powerful witness in that city to deserve such a curse upon it. Today, Chorazin is a scene of utter desolation. Chorazin has been restored somewhat as a sign the offer of the Kingdom is still open to Israel.

Chorazin is somewhat of a mystery, because it was evidently a beautiful city, and it is amazing that it was built in a volcanic area where there was no agriculture and no water. Only Jesus mentioned Chorazin, and it was not even referred

Ruins of Chorazin

to by Josephus. We must assume its importance to the ministry of Jesus is related to in John 21:25.

A small town named Chorazin has been built by Jews in another location, but the Chorazin referred to by Jesus has not been rebuilt.

▪ ▪ ▪ ▪ ▪

That is certainly true. The Chorazin referred to by Jesus has not been rebuilt. And Capernaum is a very interesting excavation. Those who go on tour will visit it. This is the remains of the city where Jesus visited and lived for a time. But there is no city of Capernaum today, and the same is true of Bethsaida. Very little of Bethsaida has been located and uncovered. There is certainly no modern-day Bethsaida. But how do we know that the Capernaum that has been excavated is the one visited by Jesus? And how do we know that Magdala of today is the one that Jesus visited during the first century? This is something that we find quite amazing in Israel. Archaeologists and historians have been working ever since the refounding of the state of Israel to confirm where the old cities and villages were located.

When the people came back to Israel and wanted to establish a kibbutz *and start a village, they had to choose a name. They had to get permission from the Israeli government on what name to choose, and the archaeologists would then decide the name of the town or village that was once in that place. Therefore, all the towns and cities in Israel today have the biblical names that are so familiar to us.*

—Gilla

THE PALESTINE
POST

JERUSALEM
THURSDAY, APRIL 17, 1947

PRICE 15 MILS
VOL. XXII. No. 6383

JEWISH COMMUNITY IMMOBILIZED BY COUNTRY-WIDE CURFEWS

4 HANGED IN SECRET AT ACRE; FUNERAL AT SAFAD

THE PALESTINE
POST

JERUSALEM
Monday, Feb. 2, 1948
PRICE: 20 MILS
VOL. XXIII No. 6627

PALESTINE POST PRESS AND OFFICES DESTROYED

Bomb and Fire Gut Three Buildings

EXPLOSION ROCKS JERUSALEM

THE PALESTINE
POST

JERUSALEM
Thursday, Feb. 17, 1949

PRICE: 25 MILS
VOL. XXV. No. 6940

WEIZMANN FIRST PRESIDENT OF ISRAEL

Jerusalem Will Come Into Its Own

Wins over Klausner on first Ballot—83:15

THE JERUSALEM
POST

TUESDAY,
JANUARY 8, 1952

PRICE: 40 PRUTA
VOL. XXVIII. No. 7154

200 HURT AS POLICE DEFEND KNESSET FROM HERUT RIOT

Sign Number Ten

From Desolation to Productivity

The prophetic history of Israel that God gave to Moses is in itself proof that the Bible is the infallible, inspired Word of God. In Deuteronomy 28:1–6 Moses tells Israel that God has given them a good land that He has blessed so that it will produce an abundance of fruit, cattle, sheep, and crops. The condition of this blessing from God was that they would obey the Lord and His commandments. But God also revealed to Moses that times would come when they would not obey the

Open market at Tel Aviv

Law, and the consequence of Israel's sins is described in Deuteronomy 28:15–18:

> But it shall come to pass, if thou wilt not hearken unto the voice of the LORD thy God, to observe to do all his commandments and his statutes which I command thee this day; that all these curses shall come upon thee, and overtake thee: Cursed shalt thou be in the city, and cursed shalt thou be in the field. Cursed shall be thy basket and thy store. Cursed shall be the fruit of thy body, and the fruit of thy land, the increase of thy kine, and the flocks of thy sheep.

In Deuteronomy 28:52–62 Moses foretells the Roman occupation of the land and the siege of Jerusalem when the Israelites would become so hungry they would "eat the fruit of thine own body, the flesh of thy sons and of thy daughters, which the LORD thy God hath given thee, in the siege, and in the straitness, wherewith thine enemies shall distress thee" (Deuteronomy 28:53). When the Romans laid siege to Jerusalem in A.D. 70 at the time of the Passover and trapped one million Jews within the walls, food became so scarce over the ensuing months that many ate their own children. The complete account of this awful time is fully described in Josephus. And then in the concluding verses of the chapter Moses described the scattering of the Jews into all nations. In chapter twenty-nine of Deuteronomy Moses describes the result of God's curse on the land during the Diaspora:

> And that the whole land thereof is brimstone, and salt, [and] burning, that it is not sown, nor beareth, nor any grass groweth therein, like the overthrow of Sodom, and Gomorrah . . . which the LORD overthrew in his anger, and in his wrath: Even all nations shall say, Wherefore hath the LORD

> done thus unto this land? what meaneth the heat of this great anger? Then men shall say, Because they have forsaken the covenant of the LORD God of their fathers, which he made with them when he brought them forth out of the land of Egypt: For they went and served other gods, . . . And the ange. of the LORD was kindled against this land. . . .
>
> —Deuteronomy 29:23–27

It was very evident that every prophecy relating to the future of Israel from the time of Moses had been fulfilled to this date. Hosea, Amos, Isaiah, Jeremiah, Ezekiel, and most of the other minor prophets confirm and support the prophecy of Moses. The entire context of prophecy in the Old Testament, which is also confirmed in the New Testament, presents the futuristic schedule for Israel. When the Jew is absent from the land, as Moses said, the land is cursed and will not grow even enough grass for sheep. When the Jews come back to the land, God blesses it again, and the land produces its full increase as the Lord has promised:

> Thou shalt no more be termed Forsaken; neither shall thy land any more be termed Desolate: but thou shalt be called Hephzibah [my delight], and thy land Beulah [wife]: for the LORD delighteth in thee, and thy land shall be married.
>
> —Isaiah 62:4

> He shall cause them that come of Jacob to take root: Israel shall blossom and bud, and fill the face of the world with fruit.
>
> —Isaiah 27:6

It is almost beyond belief the amount of fruit, vegetables, and nuts this rocky land produces today. Every kind fruit or vegetable known to man grows in Israel with the exception of the coconut.

▪ ▪ ▪ ▪ ▪

Our agriculture is so advanced and so successful. Two percent of the people produce all this food, not only for Israel, but Europe and countries other than Europe. They depend on our melons, oranges, kiwi, strawberries, avocados, and all kinds of fruits and vegetables. It is indeed amazing how a desolate desert was turned into a blooming garden with the return of the Jewish people.

When the Jews wanted to return when the country was under the British Mandate, the British would not allow them, because they said that the land could not sustain that many people. At that time there were approximately six hundred thousand Jews and six hundred thousand Arabs, but the British said that was all the people for whom the land could provide food and shelter. After that, a Christian by the name of Clay Lowdermilkr, an engineer, wrote a pamphlet titled "Palestine: A Land of Promise," and proved that in the time of Jesus more than five million people lived on the land, even without modern irrigation and modern agriculture. So today we see Israel, a land overflowing, not only with milk and honey, but an overabundance of fruits and vegetables.

Of course, much of the fruits and vegetables are grown on the kibbutzim. *What the* kibbutzim *is doing today is privatizing. They continue to produce much farming and industry, but they are changing from a socialist format to a more private enterprise system.*

—Gilla

▪ ▪ ▪ ▪ ▪

When Mark Twain visited Israel, he wrote of his travels that it was the most God-forsaken and desolate place in the world. He remarked that why anyone would want to live in the midst of desolation was more than he could understand. It seems evident that Mark Twain did not know the prophecies, because what has happened in Israel in our life time is almost beyond belief. The blossoming of Israel and the filling of the world again with fruit, is certainly one of the most evident of all the messianic signs. It is a sign of the last days that no one, regardless of politics or religion, can dispute.

THE JERUSALEM

POST

THURSDAY,
APRIL 23, 1953

PRICE: 80 PRUTA
VOL. XXIX, No. 7547

Jordan Legion Opens Shooting War In Jerusalem, Draws Israel Fire

B.G., British Envoy View Border Tension

20 Arab Casualties Reported; Six Jewish Civilians Wounded

THE JERUSALEM

POST

THURSDAY,
MARCH 18, 1954

PRICE: 100 PRUTA
VOL. XXX, No. 7820

11 Bus Passengers Are Massacred By Arab Marauders on Negev Road

Attack a 'Clear Warlike Act' | *VICTIMS CAUGHT IN AMBUSH*

THE JERUSALEM

POST

MONDAY,
NOVEMBER 15, 1954

PRICE: 100 PRUTA
VOL. XXX, No. 8015

Nagib Ousted for Alleged Part in Anti-Junta Plot

THE JERUSALEM

POST

WEDNESDAY,
SEPTEMBER 28, 1955

PRICE: 100 PRUTA
VOL. XXXI, No. 8300

Israel, Egypt Ready To Withdraw from Nitzana

But Israel Wants Assurances

THE JERUSALEM 8 Pages

POST

FRIDAY,
JULY 27, 1956

PRICE: 200 PRUTA
VOL. XXXII, No. 8565

Nasser Nationalizes Suez Canal; Says Income Will Help Build Aswan Dam

Sign Number Eleven

Irrigation

In this chapter on messianic signs in Israel today, we will consider the eleventh sign, the messianic sign of irrigation. In our previous chapter concerning God's blessing on the land when the Jews return, we mentioned the many fruits and vegetables now grown on farms that were desert just a few years ago. One vegetable item that was not grown in Israel until recently was the avocado. Avocados have always been foreign to the Middle East.

■ ■ ■ ■ ■

Avocados grow on trees that are native to Central America. When the Jews came and reclaimed the land, they tried growing again the fruits and vegetables that were grown in other countries. Avocados seemed to agriculture experts a very viable and nutritious fruit, or vegetable as some thought of it. So Jewish fruit growers went to America and brought back with them avocado seedling plants. There were several varieties of avocados, so the two that were best suited were chosen for the orchards. At first the Jewish people did not take to avocados with any great relish, so how to market them? The United States had plenty of avocados, and so did New Zealand and Australia. But Europe had no avocados, and most Europeans had never eaten them. So chefs from Israel would go to France,

Valley of Jezreel as seen from Mount Carmel

Germany, and other European countries, and teach Europeans how to prepare and serve this very good, nourishing food. Europeans now think the avocado is the best fruit or vegetable under the sun, and Israel is only too happy to provide them.

—Gilla

▪ ▪ ▪ ▪ ▪

I was amazed to see how much larger the avocado trees in Israel are compared with those in the United States or Central America. Also, the avocados grown in Israel are much larger, and this is just another example of the messianic sign of this tiny nation filling the earth with fruit.

Of course, the tremendous crops of fruits and vegetables in Israel would not be possible without irrigation, and Israel has the best and most efficient system in the world. Also, even irrigation in Israel fulfills a messianic prophecy.

> In that day will I raise up the tabernacle of David that is fallen, and close up the breaches thereof; and I will raise

> up his ruins, and I will build it as in the days of old: . . . Behold, the days come, saith the LORD, that the plowman shall overtake the reaper, and the treader of grapes him that soweth seed; and the mountains shall drop sweet wine, and all the hills shall melt. . . . And I will plant them upon their land, and they shall no more be pulled up out of their land which I have given them, saith the LORD thy God.
>
> —Amos 9:11, 13, 15

In this prophecy we see again that certain developments on the land are to be considered a sign that the restoration of the kingdom of Israel and the closing of the gap between God and His earthly people is at hand. This sign means of course that Jews must be back in the land. But Amos said that something would be taking place on the land that had never happened before. Some would be preparing the land for planting on one side of the field; some would be gathering the harvest in the middle of the field; and some would be planting on the far side of the field. Amos clearly described crop rotation. The rainy seasons in Israel are from the middle of November until April. Six months out of the year the weather is hot and dry in Israel. Without irrigation this prophecy could not be fulfilled. Because the land is so rich and

Cotton being harvested in Israel

God has blessed it, farmers in Israel now grow three crops a year. Such a thing has never been possible before. It is an important sign that the messianic age is near; which means also that the translation of the church at the Rapture must be even nearer.

▪ ▪ ▪ ▪ ▪

Irrigation is very important in Israel, because water is so scarce. We read in Deuteronomy 11:10–16:

> *For the land, whither thou goest in to possess it, is not as the land of Egypt, from whence ye came out, where thou sowedst thy seed, and wateredst it with thy foot, as a garden of herbs: But the land, whither ye go to possess it, is a land of hills and valleys, and drinketh water of the rain of heaven: A land which the LORD thy God careth for: the eyes of the LORD thy God are always upon it, from the beginning of the year even unto the end of the year. And it shall come to pass, if ye shall hearken diligently unto my commandments which I command you this day, to love the LORD your God, and to serve him with all your heart and with all your soul, That I will give you the rain of your land in his due season, the first rain and the latter rain, that thou mayest gather in thy corn, and thy wine, and thine oil. And I will send grass in thy fields for thy cattle, that thou mayest eat and be full. Take heed to yourselves, that your heart be not deceived, and ye turn aside, and serve other gods, and worship them.*

Egypt has one of the three largest rivers in the world, the Nile. With canals and water wheels, the people had no problem—there was plenty of water for crops. But the land which God gave them had only one river, the Jordan. It was a small river separated from over ninety percent of Israel by hills and mountains. In those days there were no electric pumps to take the water through pipes or canals. Moses cautioned Israel to fear the Lord and keep His commandment or He would withhold the rains.

Water management and water distribution is crucial to be able to live in the land of Israel. When Israelis rely on God's instructions and care for each other and practice water management, there is enough water. An important part of water management is drip irrigation. Through the country the tourist will see long lines of plastic pipes. Every plant is watered individually so that the water goes directly to the roots and is not wasted needlessly through evaporation. Also, along with the water the farmers put into the pipes pesticides and fertilizers. The irrigation system is run by computers that allow just the right amount of water, fertilizers, and pesticides. An example of the efficiency of the Israeli irrigation system is cotton. Israel gets thirty percent more cotton per acre than farmers in the southern part of the United States. This efficiency also refers to fruits and vegetables. Our irrigation system also helps with crop rotation, and as Amos prophesied, the plows overtake the reapers and the reapers overtake the sowers.

—Gilla

THE JERUSALEM
POST

FRIDAY, OCTOBER 5, 1956 — PRICE: 200 PRUTA — VOL. XXXII, No. 8621*

Israel Again Asks To Attend U.N. Session

THE JERUSALEM
POST

FRIDAY, NOVEMBER 2, 1956 — PRICE: 200 PRUTA — VOL. XXXII, No.8645*

EGYPT'S SINAI ARMY IN FULL FLIGHT

U.K., French Navies Converging on Suez

Eden Says Action 'Police Operation'

Israel Forces Seal Off Gaza Strip

Israelis Bag 100 Tanks

THE JERUSALEM
POST

WEDNESDAY, JULY 16, 1958 — VOL. XXXIV. No.9170 — PRICE: 150 PRUTA

French and British Units Stand By in Mid-East As U.S. Marines Land in Lebanon, Take Over Airport

B-G Warns of 'Grave Events'

THE JERUSALEM
POST

Eichmann Found by Security Services; To be Tried Here for Crimes Against Jews

THE JERUSALEM
POST

2.45 A.M.

TWELVE PAGES

FRIDAY, JUNE 1, 1962 • 28 Iyar, 5722 • 28 Zai Alhaj, 1381 — PRICE: 45 AGORA

EICHMANN HANGED

ADOLF EICHMANN—TERMED BY THE SUPREME COURT A PRIME MOVER IN THE NAZI HOLOCAUST IN WHICH SIX MILLION JEWS WERE MURDERED—WAS HANGED LAST NIGHT. HE WAS INFORMED OF THE TIME OF HIS EXECUTION EARLIER IN THE DAY. SHORTLY BEFORE 11 O'CLOCK LAST NIGHT, IT WAS ANNOUNCED THAT PRESIDENT BEN-ZVI HAD DECIDED NOT TO EXERCISE HIS PREROGATIVE TO GRANT EICHMANN CLEMENCY.

Sign Number Twelve

The Trees of Israel

Moses warned the Israelites before they crossed over the Jordan that water would be scarce and there would be only one rainy season. In 1400 B.C. at the time of the exodus, there were forests in Israel, especially in the north. The forests and groves of Israel are mentioned many times in Isaiah, Jeremiah, and Ezekiel. But the best lumber for building purposes came from Lebanon. However, Solomon planted trees throughout much of Israel.

We read about Solomon's environmental project in Ecclesiastes 2:4–6:

Acacia tree in Israel desert

> I made me great works; I builded me houses; I planted me vineyards: I made me gardens and orchards, and I planted trees in them of all kind of fruits: I made me pools of water, to water therewith the wood that bringeth forth trees.

The tribe of Dan was given the land between the section allotted to the tribe of Judah and the Mediterranean. However, this land had few trees and very little water. In addition, the Danites had to continually fight the Philistines. So finally, the entire tribe moved to the area in the north along the Dan River. They developed the city of Dan where there were many trees, some parts a veritable jungle. The fact that the tribe of Dan did not have faith to claim the land God gave them may be one reason why the scriptures indicate Dan's part in the messianic Kingdom may be small. In any event, we know that for large trees to grow in Israel in areas south of the Sea of Galilee they had to be watered during the dry season.

The destruction of Israel's forests began in A.D. 70 with Titus. According to Josephus, so many Jews were crucified during the siege of Jerusalem that there was not enough room for crosses nor wood enough to crucify those Titus condemned to death (*Fausett's Dictionary,* 145). Even the olive trees on Mount Olivet were used for crosses. According to Josephus, the Romans lay siege to Jerusalem at the time of the Passover when the number in the city would have been three times the regular population. Josephus estimated that there were two million, five hundred thousand Jews in the city at the time, not counting foreigners, lepers, or women in their monthly cycle (*Wars of the Jews,* book. VI, chapter. 9). One million, one hundred thousand died in the siege, mostly by starvation. After the city fell, the priests and Levites pleaded for their lives, but Titus concluded that as the Temple had been destroyed, there was no need for them, so he ordered their throats to be cut. Next, Titus ordered all the elderly and sick to be killed. According to Josephus, the Roman soldiers killed so many with their swords they could no longer lift their arms. Titus saved some of the best looking and tallest Jews to be bound as captives and be a part of the parade when he made his triumphant entry into Rome. Titus sent ninety-seven thousand who were still able to work into the mines in Egypt. The rest he sent to be sold on the slave markets in Alexandria, or to the many theatres throughout the Roman Empire to die as gladiators or to fight with wild beasts for the entertainment of Roman citizens (*Wars of the Jews,* book VI, chapter 9).

The Romans were unmerciful to those who opposed them, and this is why the defenders of Gamla and Masada committed suicide rather than surrender. While Josephus attempted to present Titus as a just and honorable man, it is difficult to justify his acts of extreme cruelty, especially the crucifixion of thousands of Jews daily during the siege. The reason for presenting these specific incidents in the account of the fall of Jerusalem is that the trees of Israel symbolically represented their long sufferings from A.D. 70 until the return. The Romans cut down the trees of Israel for crosses and war machines like the battering rams and catapults. The Muslims cut down the trees to build their mosques; the Crusaders cut down the trees for fire wood and to use in the construction of their castles. The Turks cut down the trees to use as ties for their railroads and firewood to stoke their engines. When the Jews began to return at the turn of the century there were no trees on the mountains and only a few in cities like Jericho. But we read this messianic promise:

> But thou, Israel, art my servant, Jacob whom I have chosen, the seed of Abraham my friend. Thou whom I have taken from the ends of the earth, and called thee from the

> chief men thereof, and said unto thee, Thou art my servant; I have chosen thee, and not cast thee away. Fear thou not; for I am with thee: be not dismayed; for I am thy God: I will strengthen thee; yea, I will help thee; yea, I will uphold thee with the right hand of my righteousness. . . . I will plant in the wilderness the cedar, the shittah tree, and the myrtle, and the oil tree; I will set in the desert the fir tree, and the pine, and the box tree together: That they may see, and know, and consider, and understand together, that the hand of the LORD hath done this, and the Holy One of Israel hath created it.
>
> —Isaiah 41:8–10, 19–20

Isaiah prophesied that God would never ultimately forsake Israel. A sign to Israel at the return would be the reforestation of the bare hills and valleys of the land. When the nations would see the myrtle tree, the oil tree, the fir trees, the pine trees, when the nations of the world would see trees growing in the mountains of Israel in such numbers and kinds that have never grown there before, they were to know, consider, and understand, that this is the Lord's doing. It is a sign to the nations that the times of the Gentiles are coming to an end, and God is once more preparing Israel for its role in the coming messianic Kingdom. Our ministry has planted two forests in Israel, one in the Valley of Elah where David slew Goliath. On every mission tour to Israel we try to give the members an opportunity to plant a tree in Israel.

▪ ▪ ▪ ▪ ▪

It is absolutely true that the mountains of Israel are now covered with trees, the majority planted and nurtured to maturity since Israel became a nation in 1948. Of course, trees are con-

tinually being planted and some are only knee-high to shoulder–high. But it is marvelous that tour groups like yours who come to visit Israel have planted millions of these trees. In addition, there are millions of every kind of fruit tree and orchard in the world all over the country. There are huge forests of date palms growing in the Dead Sea area and in the Arava (Syrian-African rift) down to Eilat where trees have never grown before. All of these orchards and all the forests now growing on the mountains and in the valleys have aided in environmental conditions that help to increase rainfall, the temperature, and the humidity. Every tree expels water into the atmosphere every day. As Isaiah said, this is a miracle, and a significant sign to the world that God is blessing Israel.

It is the Jewish National Fund that is responsible for planting trees. The Fund was created in 1901 during the fifth Zionist Congress in Basle, Switzerland. This was one of the most important decisions taken during this congress, and the JNF had a double purpose: first to buy and reclaim land in Palestine, and then to prepare it for farming and forestation. A variety of trees were planted on a trial and error basis. Jerusalem pines and pignolia pines were successful in the Judean Hills. Eucalyptus was imported from Australia early on, with the thought it would drink the water of the swamps that were prevalent in the Jezreel Valley and on the coastal plane. The swamps were not completely drained in this manner; it still took hard work to provide for adequate drainage, but the eucalyptus was so successful it was used subsequently in many other parts of the country and you still see casurinas.

In the eighties came an era of diversifying the forests. As you travel through Israel you can easily recognize the JNF forestation: it is mostly pine. The trouble is that when a disease hits the pines, they all die, and that happened in the past in Galilee, on Mount Carmel, and in the Judean hills.

When the forest is renewed we now have a greater variety of trees that include lots of oak, terebinth, and even olive trees. By now there have been more than seventy million trees planted, and planting continues vigorously. One of the latest projects is planting savannas in the Negev, the south of Israel. At first no one believed you could have trees in the Negev, but after trying we now have one of the most beautiful forests in Yatir, near the town of Arad. This is truly the desert blossoming.

Forestation keeps the soil from being washed away to the sea. It is also a help for security, and rows of trees provide good cover for patrols traveling on a border road. In the fifty years since Israel was established, we went from fourteen thousand acres of forested area to two hundred fifty thousand acres. In the fifties, the pace of forestation was twenty-five hundred acres per year, whereas now it is over six thousand a year. With it we learned that the density of twelve hundred trees per acre was too much, and now there are only four hundred to four hundred eighty trees per acre. Modern techniques allow most of the planting to be successful.

—Gilla

Sign Number Thirteen

The Vultures of Israel

For centuries there were no vultures in Israel and very few other kinds of birds. The reason for this was simple; the forests had been destroyed and there was very little grass and other types of foliage. God made the vultures for a reason. That reason was to eat animals that had died and therefore keep the land clean of garbage and disease. However, when there are no animals to die, there are no vultures. Today in Israel, on the east side of the land of Gadarenes and the lower levels of the Golan Heights at Gamla, there are hundreds and perhaps even thousands of vultures.

It is symbolic that Gamla is where the vultures nest and raise their young. Gamla was built in the fork of a deep canyon, which is one thousand feet deep. From the side of the canyon there is a land protrusion called the "Camel Hump." Some of those who returned from Babylon built a small city on the Camel Hump because below was water, and the site was easily defended.

When Josephus began the rebellion against the Romans in A.D. 66 in Galilee, his defense line was anchored on the west by Mount Tabor and on the east by Gamla. When the Roman army commanded by General Vespasian moved against Gamla, the people of the area fled to the city, increasing population greatly. Josephus himself in *The Wars of the Jews,* book four, chapter one, gave a description of Gamla and how he built up the defenses. He also gave a detailed description of the battle. Vespasian's first attempt to take the city ended in disaster, and he lost a large number of his soldiers. He called up reinforcements and finally took Gamla, killing four thousand Jews in the battle. The women and children, seeing that the battle was lost, threw themselves into the canyon below. The number who committed suicide at Gamla was said by Josephus to have been five thousand.

Vulture in the land of Israel

Vespasian's son, Captain Titus, was in command of the assault on Mount Tabor. Again, according to Josephus, the women and children taken at Mount Tabor stretched out for two miles along the road, the number totaling nine thousand. Titus commanded his soldiers to begin killing them, and six thousand women and children were killed by the swords. He evidently spared three thousand as an act of mercy. But this is why the Jews would commit suicide rather than surrender to the Romans. It is symbolic as well as prophetic that the vultures have returned to Gamla. Isaiah placed the return of the vultures to Israel in a messianic setting:

> Come near, ye nations, to hear; and hearken, ye people: let the earth hear, and all that is therein; the world, and all

> things that come forth of it. For the indignation of the LORD is upon all nations, and [his] fury upon all their armies: he hath utterly destroyed them, he hath delivered them to the slaughter. Their slain also shall be cast out, and their stink shall come up out of their carcases, and the mountains shall be melted with their blood. . . . For it is the day of the LORD'S vengeance, and the year of recompences for the controversy of Zion. . . . There shall the great owl make her nest, and lay, and hatch, and gather under her shadow: there shall the vultures also be gathered, every one with her mate.
>
> —Isaiah 34:1–3, 8, 15

During the spring and fall migration seasons, billions of birds fly through Israel, because Israel is a natural land bridge between Africa and Europe and Asia. This is one reason why we might conclude that the battle of Armageddon will be in the spring or fall. We read about the armies of the nations who will be killed at Armageddon in Revelation chapter nineteen:

Gamla Nature Park

> And I saw an angel standing in the sun; and he cried with a loud voice, saying to all the fowls that fly in the midst of heaven, Come and gather yourselves together unto the supper of the great God; . . . and all the fowls were filled with their flesh.
>
> —Revelation 19:17, 21

Many kinds of predatory birds like eagles, crows, gulls, blue jays, and others eat meat. Doubtless, the vultures will also be involved in the aftermath of Armageddon.

The Scriptures indicate to us that the battle of Ezekiel chapters thirty-eight and thirty-nine will also be during the Tribulation period, or the time of Jacob's trouble. Ezekiel 39:17 indicates that many during this invasion from the north will fall upon the Golan Heights, the biblical land of Bashan:

> . . . thus saith the Lord GOD; Speak unto every feathered fowl, and to every beast of the field, Assemble yourselves, and come; gather yourselves on every side to my sacrifice that I do sacrifice for you, even a great sacrifice upon the mountains of Israel, that ye may eat flesh, and drink blood. Ye shall eat the flesh of the mighty, and drink the blood of the princes of the earth, of rams, of lambs, and of goats, of bullocks, all of them fatlings of Bashan.
>
> —Ezekiel 39:17–18

It is interesting that the vulture population is exploding in the foothills of the mountains of Bashan, now known as the Golan Heights. The Israeli air force will not allow planes or helicopters to fly over Gamla during the vulture's nesting seasons.

It is interesting that Israel has almost adopted the vulture as its national bird. Perhaps this is because at the battle of

Armageddon the vulture will be the winged messenger of revenge for all that the Jews have suffered. It is also interesting that prior to the battle of Armageddon that vultures will be nesting in Israel, every one with their mate. The overseer of the Gamla Park told me personally that the vultures were not only laying twice as many eggs as they usually do, but they are laying four times as many. I am going to defer to Gilla for verification.

▪ ▪ ▪ ▪ ▪

I do not believe the Gamla Park Authority was exaggerating. The Gamla River with its canyons is the home of the largest number of birds of prey. The river provides a perfect habitat for nesting because of the many hiding places and availability of food. Every year forty or fifty couples of various birds of prey nest here; of that number twenty to thirty are griffon vultures. In addition, there are short-toed eagles, Egyptian vultures, Bonelli's eagles, kestrel falcons, and at night one can spot eagle owls.

The most impressive beyond any doubt is the griffon vulture. Its wingspan reaches nine feet and enables the bird to hover in place for a long time while looking for food. This vulture can weigh up to twenty-two pounds. Its color is brown, and when it is mature there are speckles of black on the wings. At the age of five or six the vulture reaches maturity and can start to reproduce. These birds stay in flocks, and they are faithful to their friends as well as to their homes. They can accumulate up to five pounds of meat in their stomach, and thus do not need to eat again for a day or two. The nesting period is in the fall, and then one can see in the air beautiful courting dances of the couples. Both partners build the nest and both share in the setting of the eggs until they hatch. The parents are very devoted. They feed the young ones and protect them with their bodies from cold and heat. The young vulture will stay in the nest almost four months before it flies away and becomes independent (Gamla Nature and Landscape, *Ofer and Liora Bahat, 1991, 64–66).*

A visit to Gamla is always a highlight. In the afternoon there are usually a great number of birds that come out and fly over the antiquities and over the canyon. This, and the many other animals that have returned to Israel, is another sign that Israel is being restored. The birds and wild animals were absent from the land for many, many centuries, but now that they are back, the land again is becoming what God wanted it to be. As far as the vultures are concerned, they are an unbelievable phenomenon.

There was a new project inaugurated in Israel two years ago sponsored by our electric company. Some vultures were fitted with positional microphones. The microphones allow scientists to follow the movements of the vultures. One of them reached as far as Istanbul, Turkey, in two days. This is a distance of several hundred miles. Some of the vultures were running away, abandoning their nests, and some were found dead. The Golan Heights is a major area of military activity. On occasion, the vultures would swallow pieces of ammunition, or they would eat meat that had been killed with bullets. So the electric company, along with the Nature Preservation Society, made feeding stations for them and gave them good quality food. Now they are doing well in Gamla. The vulture population is exploding, and they are a joy to see.

You know, Israel is a very small country—only two hundred fifty miles long and just over sixty miles wide. This is a major problem for the air force, and the pilots always joke that they can't push the gas pedal to the ground because they'll be right outside of Israeli territory. Lots of training has to happen over the Golan Heights, and the helicopters in particular need to train in the ravines. The pilots also like to go into the canyons and "play." However, just as Dr. Hutchings said, there are explicit instructions from the air force commander that forbid flying over Gamla or any other nesting areas. The rangers of the Nature Society have an open direct line to the commander to report any violations.

—Gilla

Israel smashes Arabs in Six Day War

Israeli tanks storm into action in the arid land around Rafa junction.

June 28. Israel bore the fruit of its victory over its Arab enemies in the Six Day War today. The city of Jerusalem was formally reunited under Israeli control. Jews streamed into the walled Old City, which was controlled by Jordan before the war. Many of them wept openly. Soldiers armed with machine guns and grenades bent in prayer before the Wailing Wall. The man who led Israel to glorious victory over Egypt and its Arab allies, Defense Minister Moshe Dayan, told the soldiers, "We have returned to the holiest of our holy places, never to depart from it again."

The biggest loser of this war is Egypt. Its army and air force were humiliated by Israel. Gamal Abdel Nasser gambled and he lost. Even U Thant, the usually neutral Secretary General of the United Nations, blamed Egypt for the build-up which led to the outbreak of hostilities on the 5th. Thant stopped short of saying who actually fired the first shot early that Monday morning. Israel and Egypt are still blaming each other.

Israel met strong resistance from Egyptian forces in the opening hours of the fighting. The tide turned quickly however, and within 72 hours, it was a rout. Israeli forces swept through Gaza and catapulted across the Sinai peninsula all the way to the Suez Canal. Paratroopers and naval units overran Sharm el Sheikh and broke Egypt's blockade of the Gulf of Aqaba and the port of Elath. "The strait of Tiran is now open," said Itzhak Rabin, Israeli chief of staff.

On the first day of fighting, the Israelis destroyed 50 Egyptian tanks, many of them Russian-built. On Tuesday, another 150 were disabled in the Sinai. More than 400 of Nasser's planes were shot down. "This is beyond my wildest dreams," Mordechai Hod, an air force commander, said. He called Israeli pilots "the best in the world. We made mincemeat of their air forces. We are now making mincemeat of everything on the ground."

Jordan, Nasser's latest ally, was pleading for mercy by Tuesday. Jerusalem had fallen. So had Bethlehem and Jericho. The West Bank of the Jordan River was in Israeli hands. Most of Jordan's soldiers had become Israel's prisoners.

On Israel's northern front, Syrian artillery pounded several Israeli towns in the first three days of the war. Israel denied a Syrian claim that it had captured Shear-Yashuv and was advancing on Safad. Rabin's forces struck back ferociously, and by Saturday, they rolled over the top of the Golan Heights, Syria's staging grounds for attacks into northern Israel. "If you ask me, we will never give back this ridge," said one Israeli. Some observers say the Israeli tanks could have rolled all the way to Damascus, but they stopped at El Quneitra. A cease-fire was signed on Sunday the 11th.

This war was an enormous victory for Israel, but a defeat without honor for the Arab world. Political problems led to the war. New political problems have been created. Israeli forces now occupy territories four times bigger than Israel itself. In the larger international arena, the United States and the United Arab Republic broke diplomatic relations after Nasser charged that American planes attacked his country. The United States denied the charge. All these problems have to be solved somewhere. The United Nations was virtually powerless in these six days in June (→ 7/2).

Israeli gunners on Suez patrol.

An Arab peasant pleads for peace.

Sign Number Fourteen

Wild Animal Life

In this chapter we will consider the return of wild animal life to Israel. In the previous chapter we discussed the return of the vultures, as well as bird life in general, to Israel. The prophetic Word indicates that wild animals, as mentioned in the Bible, would also return. During the Diaspora not only were there no vultures in Israel and very few birds, wild animal life became practically extinct.

In the Old Testament, lions are mentioned over one hundred times, so we know there must have been lions in Israel. We read in Judges 14:8 that Samson killed a lion with his bare hands in Gaza, which would have been near the Mediterranean Sea and the Egyptian border. So if there were lions in Gaza, we know there must have been lions throughout the country. Jeremiah mentioned that it would be impossible for a leopard to change its spots, so we know there were leopards. Leopards are referred to in books other than Jeremiah. Wild goats (or ibex) and camels are mentioned; Job and Jeremiah mention ostriches; there were hares, or rabbits; coneys; wild ox, probably meaning wild water buffalo; fox; wolves; wild dogs (these were probably the dogs with round ears, not pointed ears); deer; bear; wild boar; weasels, and perhaps a few others mentioned in Scripture where the contemporary identification might be in doubt. Tile in a Byzantine church floor in Mount Nebo, dating to the fifth century, also shows giraffes and elephants, but it is difficult to find these animals identified by their names in the Old Testament.

With the Jews returning to Israel and the ecology of the land slowly being restored, wild animal life also began to return. We read in Ezekiel 39:17: ". . . Speak unto every feathered fowl, and to every beast of the field, . . . that ye may eat flesh, and drink blood." The invasion from the north prophesied by Ezekiel is to occur after the Jews have returned to the land in "the latter years." This battle has to occur when there are wild beasts in Israel.

In the last two chapters of Isaiah the prophet looked forward to the final restoration of Israel, the coming of the Lord in fiery judgment, and the messianic blessings upon all the people of Israel alive when the promised Kingdom arrives:

> And I will rejoice in Jerusalem, and joy in my people: and the voice of weeping shall be no more heard in her, nor the voice of crying. . . . The wolf and the lamb shall feed together, and the lion shall eat straw like the bullock: and dust shall be the serpent's meat. They shall not hurt nor destroy in all my holy mountain, saith the LORD.
>
> —Isaiah 65:19, 25

According to a new book, *The Biotech Century,* by Jeremy Rifkin, unbelievable things are now happening in genetic engineering with recombining DNA. It is now possible for pigs to grow human hearts; cows to give mothers' milk; mix a firefly with a tobacco plant and the plant glows in the dark; and it is even possible to produce a lion that will eat straw instead of meat. We have no idea if this was some scientific development that Isaiah was referring to, or if he was only referring to the messianic age in a symbolic sense when there would be complete peace on earth. However, some of the prophecies of the Bible relating to the messianic age could not be completed without the return of animal life as it was in Old Testament times.

At Gamla we have also seen fox, deer, ibex, coneys, and rabbits. One day I believe I saw a wolf. At Ein Gedi there are several types of animals in evidence, including deer, ibex, coneys, and there is a sign warning tourists what to do in the event they meet a leopard. We have not heard of any lions or bears back in the land, but with the restoration of the ecology this too is possible.

▪ ▪ ▪ ▪ ▪

The last time a lion was noticed in Israel was 1960. The American archaeologist Nelson Gluck was fortunate to see a lion on the shores of the Jordan.

It is certainly true that all the animals you have mentioned are back in the land with the restoration of the ecology. And yes, there are many leopards in Israel today. Many of them do come to Ein Gedi for water. This was the place used by David for he and his men to hide from Saul. There is plenty of water, plenty of ibex and deer for meat, and caves to sleep in. The waterfall comes from springs that flow between Ein Gedi and Jerusalem all the year long.

At a safari reserve north of Eilat there has been a program developing to bring all the animals mentioned in the Bible back to Israel. All the animals in Israel mentioned in the Bible that are still missing are being brought to this area, and when there are a sufficient number of all these animals, they will be released in different parts of the country, and then all the biblical animals will be back in the land.

Many of the animals have to be purchased or captured from farther down in Africa. This effort has now been continu-

ing for the past fifteen to twenty years. However, they are confident that all the animals mentioned in the Bible will be back in the land, and this definitely will be a fulfillment of prophecy.

—Gilla

Animals being restored to Israel

At Ein Gedi a sign is posted warning tourists what to do in the event they meet a leopard

Camels are very common in the Middle East

The last time a lion was spotted in Israel was in 1960 by American archaeologist Nelson Gluck

We have seen many fox at Gamla, as well as deer, ibex, coneys, and rabbits.

Wild goats—another common sight in the Middle East—used by Bedouins for tent-making and food.

At Ein Gedi, there are several types of animals in evidence. Dr. Hutchings believes he once saw a wolf there.

Although we have not heard of any bears back in the land, with the restoration of the ecology this too is possible.

THE JERUSALEM

POST

MONDAY, JANUARY 6, 1964 • 21 Tevet, 5724 • 21 Sha'aban, 1383

POPE PAUL, RELAXED AND HAPPY, SPENDS 'UNFORGETTABLE DAY' AS PILGRIM IN ISRAEL

Pope Paul VI concluded a day-long visit to Israel at 9.07 p.m. last night, when he crossed the Mandel baum Gate into Jordan after a pilgrimage that ranged from Galilee to Judea. Before taking final leave of President Zalman Shazar in Jerusalem, the Pope expressed his full awareness of the freedom and equality enjoyed by the Catholic Church here. The Pontiff was replying to a farewell speech by the President, in which Mr. Shazar once again noted that Israel's hand "is stretched out in gesture of peace towards the neighbouring states, and our eyes lifted in search of true peace in the world . . . based on trust and respect among peoples."

THE JERUSALEM

POST

WEDNESDAY, MAY 19, 1965 • 17 Iyar, 5725 • 18 Muharram, 1385

Syria hangs Eli Cohen in public square, as spy

Sense of shock and outrage in Jerusalem

ISRAELI DENIED DEFENCE

SCOPUS ROAD OPENED,

THE JERUSALEM

POST

Published in Jerusalem, Israel, daily except on Saturday by The Palestine Post Ltd. Founded in 1932 by Gershon AGRON. Registered at the G.P.O. Copyright of all material reserved; reproduction permitted only by arrangement. Editor: TED R. LURIE.

Jerusalem: 9 Rehov Havatselet, P.O.B. 81, Telephone [illegible] · Tel Aviv: [illegible] Rehov Nahlat Binyamin, P.O.Box 1125, Tel. [illegible] · Haifa: [illegible] Rehov Herzl, Hadar Hacarmel, P.O.Box [illegible], Telephone [illegible]

OTHER WAR NEWS, pages 2, 3, 4

PRICE : 35 AGORA

WEDNESDAY, JUNE 7, 1967 • EYAR 28, 5727 • SAFAR 29, 1387 • VOL. XXXVII, No. 11979

OLD CITY ENCIRCLED; 200 EGYPTIAN TANKS SMASHED; GAZA FALLS

Syrian attacks repulsed

Sign Number Fifteen

Increasing Rainfall

As we have noted previously, the Bible states without qualification that when the Jew is in the land of promise God blesses it; when the Jew is absent from the land, God curses it and it becomes barren and desolate. This was the condition of the entire country during the Diaspora.

The literal reason why the land became an object of remorse and desolation was that the rains became less and less the longer the Jews were scattered over the world. However, every major prophet and many of the minor prophets foretold that when the Jews began to return to the land in anticipation of the messianic age the rains would also begin to increase once more.

The book of Joel is about the coming Day of the Lord in which the nations will be judged during a time of tribulation, which would end with the annihilation of Israel's enemies.

> Blow ye the trumpet in Zion, and sound an alarm in my holy mountain: let all the inhabitants of the land tremble: for the day of the LORD cometh, for it is nigh at hand; . . . Be glad then, ye children of Zion, and rejoice in the LORD your God: for he hath given you the former rain moderately, and he will cause to come down for you the rain, the former rain, and the latter rain in the first month.
>
> —Joel 2:1, 23

In Bible times there were two seasons of rain in Israel: the fall and winter. During the Diaspora, as the Lord said, there was little rain. The average rainfall between 1931 and 1960 in the northern half of Israel was 21.1 inches a year. In 1980 the average rainfall in Israel was 29.1 inches, an increase of approximately forty percent. The amazing phenomenon about the rainfall increase is that the percentage of increase has matched the percentage of increase in Jewish population during the past seventy years.

Ninety percent of the water needs of Israel come from the Sea of Galilee, a relatively small body of water approximately five miles wide and thirteen miles long. Without the Sea of Galilee, there would be no Israel. Yet, the Sea of Galilee remains full. The water is very clean and pure, and even as the Jewish and Palestinian populations of Israel have increased from one million to seven million, there is enough water for industry, household, and irrigation usage.

Although ninety percent of the water needs of Israel come from the Sea of Galilee (a relatively small body of water), the sea remains full. As the population of Israel has increased, so too has the average rainfall.

The prophet Hosea also prophesied that the former rains and the latter rains would be restored to Israel in the time the Messiah would appear.

Then shall we know, if we follow on to know the LORD: his going forth is prepared as the morning;

> and he shall come unto us as the rain, as the latter and former rain unto the earth.
>
> —Hosea 6:3

The reason the Sea of Galilee has remained so unpolluted over the thousands of years is due to Lake Huleh. Lake Huleh is actually a swamp. The Jordan River is fed by three tributaries, the Dan being the largest. The waters flow into the swamp of Lake Huleh about five miles north of the Sea of Galilee. As the Jordan slowly filters through the swamp, silt is removed and bacteria action purifies the water. Engineers in Israel decided they could dry up the swamp and use it for farmland, which afterward did produce good crops. However, they soon found out that God knew what He was doing when He put the swamp above the Sea of Galilee. When Huleh Lake was dried up and water from the Jordan River went directly into the Sea of Galilee, silt, muddy water, and pollution became a problem. Also, there was an explosion of the rat population in the Huleh Lake bed. So at least part of the Huleh Lake swamp was restored. It is indeed miraculous how the ecology of upper Galilee provides life saving waters for the new nation of Israel.

▪ ▪ ▪ ▪ ▪

The present rainfall in the northern half of Israel has now increased to thirty-five inches a year, which means it has more than doubled the amount at about the time that the nation was refounded in 1948. The Sea of Galilee is the major water source for Israel. It is pumped into pipes and sent to all parts of the country. Not only is the Jordan River a major source of water, so is the Golan Heights. From the highest point on the

Golan Heights the water runs westward into brooks, reaching the Jordan. This is one reason why the Golan Heights are so important to Israel. It is such an important water shed.

The Sea of Galilee serves as a natural reservoir. That part of Israel south to the Dead Sea is very dry, but water is brought by pipes to the arid and desert areas. The Sea of Galilee now provides water for all of Israel, including the West Bank, with a population of both areas approximately seven million.

Besides the Golan Heights, there is, of course, the Dan River that runs into the Jordan. The headwaters of the Dan River are just to the west of the Dan excavations. The river itself suddenly comes up out of the ground with a roar, much like a geyser. Within a few yards there is a swift, rushing river. To get to this artesian source, tourists have to go through a veritable jungle. This is certainly something that those who visit Israel do expect to see.

The waters of the Dan and Jordan rivers are connected to the snows on Mount Hermon. In the winter snows cover Mount Hermon and in the spring and summer seep into the ground and appear at lower elevations. The Dan River is one of those places and Caesarea Philippi is another. The rainy season in Israel is from November to April, but the waters from Mount Hermon and the Golan feed the Dan River the whole year. To see the Dan River with its enormous quantities of water is a precious sight. The Dan River and Mount Hermon provide the setting for Psalm 42:

> *O my God, my soul is cast down within me: therefore will I remember thee from the land of Jordan, and of the Hermonites, from the hill Mizar. Deep calleth unto deep at the noise of thy waterspouts: all thy waves and thy billows are gone over me.*

Continuing on through the nature reserve is the Dan excavations. Dan was a large city, and one of the most interesting excavations is the altar where Jereboam set up the golden calf and made Israel to sin by entering into idol worship. Also at Dan is the very gate that Abraham entered when he pursued the kings of the north to rescue Lot.

But of course the most important biblical relevance of Upper Galilee is the Sea of Galilee, and the increased rainfall which certainly has a prophetic fulfillment.

—Gilla

THE JERUSALEM

POST

Published in Jerusalem, Israel, daily except on Saturday, by The Palestine Post Ltd. Founded in 1932 by Gershon AGRON. Registered at the G.P.O. Copyright of all material reserved; reproduction permitted only by arrangement. Editor: TED R. LURIE

Jerusalem: 9 Rehov Hahavatzelet, P.O.B. 81, Telephone 28331 (8 lines) · Tel Aviv: 44 Rehov Yehuda Halevi, P.O.Box 1125, Tel. 624215 · Haifa: 34 Rehov Herzl, Hadar Hacarmel; P.O.Box 4810. Telephone 64594

THURSDAY, JUNE 6, 1968 • SIVAN 10, 5728 • RABI'A EL-AWAL 9, 1388

JORDANIAN CHARGED WITH SHOOTING ROBERT KENNEDY

THE JERUSALEM

POST

Published in Jerusalem, Israel, daily except on Saturday by The Palestine Post Ltd, Founded in 1932 by Gershon AGRON. Registered at the G.P.O. Copyright of all material reserved; reproduction permitted only by arrangement. Editor: TED R. LURIE

Jerusalem: 9 Rehov Hahavatzelet, P.O.B. 81, Telephones 24253, 24321 · Tel Aviv: 81 Rehov Nahlat Binyamin, P.O.Box 1125, Tel. 624215 · Haifa: 34 Rehov Herzl, Hadar Hacarmel, P.O.Box 4810, Telephone 64594.

THURSDAY, JUNE 15, 1967 • SIVAN 7, 5727 RABIA AWAL 8, 1387 • VOL. XXXVII, No. 11985*

200,000 at Western Wall in first pilgrimage since Dispersion

At the Western Wall — Some of the 200,000 Israelis who celebrated *Shavuot* at the wall of the Temple yesterday. (Goren photo)

THE JERUSALEM

POST

Published in Jerusalem, Israel, daily except on Saturday by The Palestine Post Ltd, Founded in 1932 by Gershon AGRON. Registered at the G.P.O. Copyright of all material reserved; reproduction permitted only by arrangement. Editor: TED R. LURIE

Jerusalem: 9 Rehov Hahavatzelet, P.O.B. 81, Telephones 24253, 24321 · Tel Aviv: 81 Rehov Nahlat Binyamin, P.O.Box 1125, Tel. 624215 · Haifa: 34 Rehov Herzl, Hadar Hacarmel; P.O.Box 4810, Telephone 64594.

THURSDAY, JUNE 29, 1967 • SIVAN 21, 5727 • RABIA AWAL 22, 1387 • VOL. XXXVII, No. 11997*

OLD-NEW JERUSALEM BORDER IS ABOLISHED

FREE MOVEMENT FROM NOON TODAY

U.S. denies Israel claim to Jerusalem

Sign Number Sixteen

Jerusalem, An International Problem

The burden of the word of the LORD for Israel, saith the LORD, which stretcheth forth the heavens, and layeth the foundation of the earth, and formeth the spirit of man within him. Behold, I will make Jerusalem a cup of trembling unto all the people round about, when they shall be in the siege both against Judah and against Jerusalem. And in that day will I make Jerusalem a burdensome stone for all people: all that burden themselves with it shall be cut in pieces,

Jerusalem as seen from the Mount of Olives

> though all the people of the earth be gathered together against it.
>
> —Zechariah 12:1–3

In March 1995 Israel observed the three thousandth anniversary of Jerusalem, founded by King David in 1005 B.C. The most important place in Jerusalem is the Temple Site, which David bought for fifty shekels of silver from Araunah, the Jebusite. The Jebusites were descendants of the Canaanites. Araunah threw in a team of oxen for good measure (2 Samuel 24).

In 600 B.C. Jerusalem and the Temple were destroyed by the Babylonians; the city and the Temple were occupied and defiled by Antiochus Epiphanes in 160 B.C.; the city and the Temple were destroyed by the Romans in A.D. 70; overrun by the Muslims in A.D. 700; taken by the Crusaders in A.D. 1100; conquered by the Turks in A.D. 1500; captured by the British in A.D. 1917. The British gave Jerusalem to the Jordanians and it was retaken by the Israelis in A.D. 1967. There has always been a controversy over Jerusalem, but never in history has the city been a burdonsome stone and a cup of trembling to "all the people of the earth" as it is today.

In Israel there are many rocks that have to be moved from farmland and to remove these heavy rocks is a great burden. Nehemiah was a cup bearer, and if the cup bearer carried a drink with poison, or had bad news to tell the king, his hands would tremble. If the king perceived the cup bearer's hand was trembling, the servant could lose his head.

After 1948 the original city of Jerusalem with the Temple Site remained in Jordanian control. In the 1967 Six-Day War, Israel occupied the old city, but the Temple Site remained in Muslim and Jordan's control. The reason for this was that the army, whose leadership was mostly secular and atheistic, did not want to be put under pressure to rebuild the Temple at that time.

Although Jerusalem has always been a site of war, strife, and controversy, only until now has it been a matter of contention for all the people of all nations. The Catholic Church has always had designs on Jerusalem. The April 3, 1993, edition of the *Jerusalem Post* carried an architectural drawing of the pope's design for a Jerusalem Vatican. The Catholic Church owns extensive properties in Jerusalem.

After Israel was refounded as an independent state in 1948, the United Nations passed Resolution 181, advocating the internationalization of Jerusalem. The international authority would supposedly be the United Nations. The U.N. did not appear overly concerned about internationalization when East Jerusalem was under Jordanian control. The main thrust for internationalization came after the 1967 war when Israel captured East Jerusalem. The internationalization issue was tied to the 1993 Oslo Agreement. Jewish leaders attempted to take this issue out of political consideration on May 29, 1993. The *Jerusalem Post* reported:

> Seventy leaders of world Jewry gathered . . . to sign the covenant, meant to express the bond between Diaspora Jews and Jerusalem as the undivided capital of Israel. The covenant . . . which was signed a year ago by Israeli leaders, and on Jerusalem Day by President Ezer Weizman—is based on biblical quotations and themes from the writings of the Sages, Jewish tradition, and Israeli law.

The effort of Yasser Arafat and the Palestinian Authority to establish an independent state has also complicated the future status of Jerusalem, because the so-called "world community of nations" supports such a goal.

Hillary Clinton has openly advocated the establishing of a Palestinian state, and it is unthinkable that she would do this without the encouragement of President Clinton. While he is reticent to take such a bold stand, he has his wife act in his place. President Clinton also sent his own three main political power movers to Israel to elect a premier who will allow a Palestinian state and possibly the internationalization of Jerusalem. A CNN report dated March 30, 1999, quotes the European Union, by unanimous vote, giving Israel one year to submit to the existence of a Palestinian state. All nations today are involved in the concerns over the future of Jerusalem. This fact is one of the most obvious messianic signs in Israel today:

> If I forget thee, O Jerusalem, let my right hand forget her cunning. If I do not remember thee, let my tongue cleave to the roof of my mouth; if I prefer not Jerusalem above my chief joy.
>
> —Psalm 137:5–6

▪ ▪ ▪ ▪ ▪

We know that in these last centuries Jerusalem was not a matter of contention until the Jews began returning to the land. After the Romans detroyed the Temple in A.D. *70 and there were several succeeding governments in Israel, no one ever thought about Jerusalem. With the Jews it was always, "Next year in Jerusalem." Jerusalem never came up in the League or Nations or international conventions. However, as more Jews came back after the Holocaust, and there were national aspirations by Israelis, the United Nations sent an envoy to discuss making Jerusalem an international city. It should not be surprising that Jerusalem today is motivating such controversy, because it is the biblical and spiritual capital of the earth. Within the city of Jerusalem is the Temple Mount with its history of the two temples. We know that in the future, according to God's Word, another Temple will stand upon the Temple Mount, and this will be the Temple of the Messiah.*

On the Temple Mount today, we have the Dome of the Rock and the El Aqsa Mosque. Just recently the mufti, *the religious Moslem authority, stated in a sermon in the mosque that the Jews have nothing to do with the Temple Mount, that it is of no interest to them. As soon as there were clear indications that the status of Jerusalem would become an important issue of the U.N., as well as between the PLO and Israel, the Vatican made known its willingness to have diplomatic relations with Israel. The Vatican has never had diplomatic relations with Israel, but as soon as the future of Jerusalem became an issue, the Vatican wants to have a say in this matter. Jerusalem is an important city to Jews, Moslems, and Christians; therefore, it is a city of great contention. Jerusalem will be an utmost issue of contention, and any proposed agreement may result in national wars and religious opposition. This is why we are admonished by the Lord in Psalm 122:6 to "pray for the peace of Jerusalem."*

The issues that are involved in varying interests and contentions over Jerusalem are intense and far-reaching. This is why the prophet said that Jerusalem would be a stone of contention.

Jerusalem is such a sensitive and politically contentious issue that only one out of one hundred and ninety-two nations is brave enough to have their embassy in Jerusalem. That nation is tiny Costa Rica. Of course, Israel wants all nations to have their embassies in Jerusalem. The time is coming when every nation will have its embassy in Jerusalem:

> *And it shall come to pass, that every one that is left of all the nations which came against Jerusalem shall even go up from year to year to worship the King, the* L*ORD of hosts, and to keep the feast of tabernacles. And it shall be, that whoso will not come up of all the families of the earth unto Jerusalem to worship the King, the* L*ORD of hosts, even upon them shall be no rain.*
>
> —*Zechariah 14:16–17*

There is one other exception to the acceptance of Jerusalem as the capital of Israel: the Christian Embassy. The Christian Embassy also organizes every year a massive pilgrimage to show support for Israel during the Feast of Tabernacles.

—*Gilla*

OLD CITY, MOST OF SINAI FALL, TIRAN OPENED

THE JERUSALEM POST

THURSDAY, JUNE 8, 1967 • EYAR 29, 5727 • RABIA AWAL 1, 1387 • VOL. XXXVII, No. 11980 PRICE: 35 AGORA

Forces near Suez, West Bank taken

After 60 hours of battle Israel forces yesterday controlled most of the West Bank of Jordan, including the Old City of Jerusalem, Nablus, Ramallah, Jericho and Bethlehem; in Sinai they cut through to the approaches of the Suez Canal and captured Sharm e-Sheikh, the Chief of Staff, Rav Aluf Yitzhak Rabin, said yesterday.

The Defence Minister, Mr. Moshe Dayan, last night declared that Israel has achieved her main political aims in this campaign. Addressing an overflow press conference at Beit Sokolow, Mr. Dayan declared that from the very onset it was Israel's objective to ensure the free passage of shipping to Eilat.

SIXTY HOURS

Moshe Dayan in the Old City.

BULLETIN:

U.N. Council's deadline for cease-fire

Premier Eshkol accompanied by Aluf Uzzi Narkiss, O.C. Central Command, at the Western Wall yesterday. (Photo Meyerowitz)

Premier, Chief Rabbis pray at Western Wall

By N. D. GROSS, Jerusalem Post Reporter

Mr. Levi Eshkol yesterday took part in afternoon prayers at the Western Wall. He was the first leader of a Jewish Government to visit the site of the Temple since its loss 1,897 years ago.

Sign Number Seventeen

Israel a Democracy

World War One was supposedly fought to make the world safe for democracy, and even today our president will make a pretense of pursuing political expedience under the guise of aiding democracies. Needless to say that in the Middle East our nation enters into political fellowship with some of the most brutal dictators who ever lived. But Israel, in fact, is the only democracy in the Middle East. We read in Zechariah 12:5–6:

> And the governors of Judah shall say in their heart, The inhabitants of Jerusalem shall be my strength in the LORD of hosts their God. In that day will I make the governors of Judah like an hearth of fire among the wood, and like a torch of fire in a sheaf; and they shall devour all the people round about, on the right hand and on the left: and Jerusalem shall be inhabited again in her own place, even in Jerusalem.

Preterists may say that this prophecy was fulfilled in A.D. 70. However, we read in the same chapter, verse eight, that God would save the feeble in that day because even a feeble person will be as strong as David. This certainly was not true in A.D. 70, as Josephus tells us that the feeble and elderly who survived the siege were all killed by Titus. Only the young and strong were kept alive.

We notice that Zechariah referred to the governors of Judah in that day. According to Hosea and other prophets, it was foretold that Israel would abide many days without a king or a prince. Isaiah had prophesied that the kings of Israel would be killed and the royal princes would be made eunuchs. The great King of Kings, the Messiah, would be born of the seed of woman as prophesied in Genesis 3:15. Jesus Christ claimed that He was the Messiah, born of a virgin, conceived by the Holy Spirit, but Israel rejected Him. The Romans appointed puppet kings of the lineage of Esau over Israel, but there was no true prince or king from the lineage of David.

The first government of Israel was a "judicial theocracy" composed of judges who governed by the Law of Moses. The second government was a "monarchy theocracy," a ruler anointed by the high priest to reign according to God's ordinances for human government.

After a remnant returned from the Babylonian captivity there was no king, so the government was evidently fashioned after the Persian government which had a representative from each of the one hundred twenty provinces. The returning Jews formed what was called the "Great Assembly" with one hundred twenty members. *Knesset* means assembly.

When Israel became a nation on May 14, 1948, a provisional state council was formed to function until the Great Assembly or Knesset members could be elected. In 1949 one hundred twenty Knesset members were elected by the citizens of Israel. The first Knesset, which was composed of multiracial representatives (including representatives of the Yemenite Jews who were returning), dealt with such issues as health, industrialization, jobs, schools, and immigration. The United Nations also delivered a referendum to the Knesset to internationalize Jerusalem, and in a speech before the Knesset on December 5, 1949, Prime Minister David Ben Gurion declared: "Jewish Jerusalem is an integral and inseparable part of the State of Israel, just as it is an inseparable part of the history of Israel, the faith of Israel, and the spirit of our people."

The prophet Zechariah foretold that when the Jews returned that the nation of Israel would be ruled by governors, indicating a democracy. Israel is today a democracy within a republic framework; in fact, Israel, as we have noted, is the only democratic government in all that area of the world. This is certainly a prophetic messianic sign.

■ ■ ■ ■ ■

Not only is Israel a democracy, we probably suffer from excess democracy. The Knesset is composed of one hundred twenty members. Members are elected every four years in general elections. Israel has twenty political parties that attempt to get representatives into the Knesset to promote and represent their political views. This makes it very difficult to form a stable

Knesset: the seat of Israeli government

government, because there is never one political party that has a majority. Intricate agreements have to be formed to develop coalitions.

There are in the Knesset various small groups to represent the populations. This could be proposed as democracy in its most possible, purest form. There are Palestinian members in the Knesset, too. Every citizen, regardless of their race, religion, or sex, has the right to vote when he or she has reached the age of eighteen. Israel has to be very careful when annexing territories. Take the example of Bethlehem. We feel that Bethlehem should be part of Israel, and the Christians in Bethlehem asked immediately after the Six-Day War to be annexed to Israel, just like Jerusalem and the Golan Heights. However, knowing the vast number of Muslims that live in the area and would come into the city for employement, and knowing the incredible birth rate of the Muslims, Israel had to decline. After all we, want to remain a Jewish country and would not like the Arabs to take over by sheer numbers.

Of course, the past several presidents of the United States have endeavored to place political pressure on the prime minister, as well as Knesset members, to interfere in both domestic policies and our relationships with the surrounding Arab nations. Many Israelis resent this, because we have elected our own government leaders to express the will of our own citizens, and not necessarily the will of the president of the United States. In spite of all this, our government agencies survive as independent functions to serve the citizens of Israel.

—Gilla

Sign Number Eighteen

Wars of Israel and Jerusalem Retaken

Another important messianic sign is also found in the prophecy of Zechariah:

> In that day will I make the governors of Judah like an hearth of fire among the wood, and like a torch of fire in a sheaf; and they shall devour all the people round about, on the right hand and on the left. . . .
>
> —Zechariah 12:6

1. This prophecy cannot refer to wars involving Israel prior to 1948. We note again that Israel, when these wars occur, will be ruled by governors, not a king or a prince. After the return of the remnant from Babylon, Israel remained militarily weak, dominated by Persia, Greece, Syria, Egypt, and Rome. Also, this prophecy could not refer to the A.D. 66–72 Jewish rebellion against Rome. Israel was the nation devoured, not all the people on the left and the right.
2. This could not be a reference to wars during the Kingdom age, because all the weapons of war will be destroyed and there will be peace for one thousand years.
3. These wars prophesied by Zechariah had to occur between

1948 and the coming of the Messiah, and several of these wars have already happened exactly as the prophet foretold.

The overwhelming victories of tiny Israel over vastly superior armies of Egypt (on the left hand) and Syria and Jordan (on the right hand) in 1948, 1967, and 1973, amazed the entire world. In addition to the exceptions noted above, Zechariah in this prophecy could not be referring to Armageddon. At the time of Armageddon only one-third of the Jews who had been living in the land will be left alive, and these will be hiding in a place of refuge, which the Bible indicates will be Petra.

War of 1948: The day after David Ben Gurion declared Israel to be an independent nation on May 14, 1948, Egyptian airplanes bombed Tel Aviv. Within the week the combined armies of Lebanon, Syria, and Iraq moved to take over the cities of the north and in the Galilee area. Experienced and battle-tested Arab forces armed by England moved across the Jordan to Jericho to occupy Bethlehem and Jerusalem. In the meantime, a large Egyptian army moved across the Sinai to occupy Gaza and take Tel Aviv. There appeared to be no way the poorly trained and equipped Jewish fighters could withstand the might of a combined army of five Arab states. General George Marshall warned Ben Gurion that the Israeli forces would be liquidated within seventy-two hours, but miraculously, Israel won, astounding world military experts. The Independence War lasted about six months.

1967 Six-Day War: Although a U.N.-arranged armistice ended the battles between Israel and the Arab alliance, the war continued on a terrorist and guerrilla basis. Between 1951 and 1955, nine hundred sixty-seven Israelis (men, women, and children) were killed in these types of attacks. In 1956 there was a brief period of hostilities involving Israeli, French, and British forces when Nasser of Egypt took sole possession of the Suez Canal. Between 1956 and 1966 terrorist attacks—the artillery shelling by the Syrians of northern Israel from high mountains on the Golan Heights—continued. The Soviet Union, attempting to put more pressure on the United States in the Middle East, heavily armed the Arab nations from Morocco to Iran, and goaded the Arab alliance to destroy Israel in a final gigantic war. Between May 30 and June 4, 1967, the combined armed forces of Egypt, Iraq, Jordan, Saudi Arabia, Kuwait, Algeria, and Lebanon invaded Israel. The tiny nation of Israel responded once more and within six days had conquered the Sinai, Golans, West Bank, and East Jerusalem, recalling the prophecy of Zechariah that in that day the weakest Jew would be stronger than King David.

Yom Kippur War: The Arab mindset accepts the historic Hannah-Elizabeth position that patience and stubborness in the end will win out. The Arabs can afford to lose ninety-nine wars—all they have to do is win the one hundredth war. Israel cannot afford to lose even one war. After the Six-Day War

Israeli Chariot tank

of 1967, the Arab nations, with Russian help, simply began to arm for the next round. October 6, 1973, was not only a Jewish sabbath, it was Yom Kippur, the most holy day in Israel. No Jew is supposed to work, eat, travel, listen to the radio, or watch television on this day. The Arabs took advantage of this knowledge about Jewish religious worship. So on this day, without warning, Egypt and Syria attacked Israel with one thousand airplanes, four thousand tanks, and eight hundred thousand men. To this force Saudi Arabia, Kuwait, and Jordan added more tanks, men, and planes. Because a large part of the Israeli army was on leave during Yom Kippur, and Israelis were not even watching television, it was difficult to marshall the nation's armed forces to defend against this overwhelming assault. When Israel finally got their defense forces to the battle fronts, the nation faced this monstrous army with only five hundred planes, seventeen hundred tanks, and three hundred thousand soldiers. Again, within two weeks, the bulk of the Arab armies were destroyed or in retreat. The Israeli armed forces could have taken Damascus or Cairo at will. Russia again threatened nuclear war, and another armistice was signed.

War memorial on Golan Heights

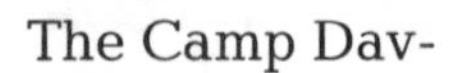
The Camp Dav-

id agreement arranged by President Jimmy Carter in 1978 returned the Sinai to Egypt in exchange for a peace treaty between Israel and Egypt. The Oslo Accord in 1993, while resulting in a peace treaty between Israel and Jordan, has created an impossible situation that can only be terminated at the battle of Armageddon.

Although in the 1967 Six-Day War Israel retook East Jerusalem, the Jerusalem of the Bible, and Jerusalem was inhabited again in its own place, Daniel prophesied that wars in Israel would continue until the Messiah would come, and so they have. Therefore, when we pray for the peace of Jerusalem as commanded in Scripture, we are really praying for the coming of Israel's Messiah, and Whom Christians know and believe is the Lord Jesus Christ.

▪ ▪ ▪ ▪ ▪

No one can understand the 1967 war unless they believe in miracles. Jordan is more friendly to Israel than any of the other Arab nations. There were even secret communications between King Abdulla, the grandfather of King Hussein, and the government of Israel. When the 1967 war broke out, it started between Israel and Egypt in the Sinai. Israel sent a message to King Hussein requesting that he not interfere and nothing would happen to Jordan. Although Israeli forces were already defeating the Egyptians, Egypt kept sending radio messages that its army was already at the gates of Tel Aviv. The Egyptian announcements of success were so convincing that Jordan was afraid that it would miss out on a great victory. The Jordanian army attacked at Jerusalem. The Jordanians were, of course, defeated and this in turn gave Israel possession of the Old City. If that is not a miracle, I do not know what is.

In 1948 the Egyptians were advancing along the coast from Gaza to Tel Aviv. Kibbutz Yad Mordecai *was just off the road. The attack began on May 16, 1948, two days after Ben Gurion declared Israel to be a sovereign state. The members of the* kibbutz *prepared defenses on high ground. With only a few dozen defenders (armed mainly with rifles), they held off the entire Egyptian army for four days. Finally, on May 20, the Egyptians brought up tanks, but even so, the defenders were able to turn the tanks back. In this attack, sixteen defenders were killed and twenty wounded. Because they were holding back entire Egyptian regiments that were attacking, a detachment of Israeli soldiers came to help. On May 23 there was a tremendous artillery shelling of the* kibbutz, *but they would not give in to the Egyptians. All the women and children were evacuated, and yet the defenders stood their ground.*

Over four hundred Egyptian soldiers were killed in the assault upon this kibbutz, *and this completely foiled the enemy's plans to quickly take Tel Aviv and completely cut off Jerusalem from supplies and reinforcements. Delaying the Egyptian advance allowed two Israeli brigades to fortify positions along the highway, and Tel Aviv remained in Jewish hands. Had Tel Aviv fallen, then there may not have been a Jewish nation today. Zechariah prophesied that in that day a feeble Jew would be stronger than David. We see again a great miracle.*

In 1948 the outcome of this war was also absolutely miraculous. There were only six hundred thousand Jews in Israel. There was no trained army. It was very difficult to obtain weapons, because the British would not allow it. Weapons had to be smuggled in from America and Czechoslovakia. And although most of the Jews were survivors of the Holocaust, Israel was attacked by armies from eight Arab countries. It would seem almost unbelievable that a few thousand Jews armed mostly with small weapons, no planes, and no tanks, could meet such overwhelmingly superior forces and survive. But Israel did win and survive, and again, there is no way to explain this but that it was a miracle.

—Gilla

AIR FORCE WINS SUPREMACY AS ARMY DRIVES EGYPTIANS BACK INTO SINAI AND GAZA

THE JERUSALEM POST

TUESDAY, JUNE 6, 1967 • EYAR 27, 5727 • SAFAR 28, 1387 • VOL. XXXVII, No. 11978 • PRICE: 35 AGORA

BULLETIN: The army spokesman announced that 374 enemy planes were destroyed yesterday. Nineteen Israeli planes were lost.

Jordan shells Jerusalem; 10 dead, houses damaged

The Israel Defence Forces yesterday morning repelled an attempted Egyptian air and tank attack and smashed into Sinai as the Israel Air Force appeared to have won total supremacy.

Before nightfall an Israeli task force had captured the key town of Khan Younis, thereby cutting off the Egyptian forces in the Gaza Strip.

(The British Broadcasting Corporation last night reported that Israel armour has sliced through the Gaza Strip to the Mediterranean and that Arab forces in the area "are no longer a fighting factor.")

At the same time, Jordanian positions yesterday morning began firing and shelling in Jerusalem and on Mt. Scopus — a battle which continued intermittently throughout the day. Effective Israel counter-action silenced most of the Jordanian positions by the end of the day. Ten civilians were killed and about a hundred wounded.

Three Syrian airplanes also went into action briefly yesterday morning, in the Megiddo area. Two were shot down.

Mediterranean Sea

Degania was shelled by both Syrian and Jordanian flat trajectory fire. The bombing in the north was mostly between Haifa and Acre, in the Bayside area. One of the targets apparently was the refinery, but was no damage caused.

Further to the south, places shelled or bombed were Megiddo, Netanya, Ramat Hakovesh, Eyal, ...

ESHKOL: ARAB AIR FORCES DEFEATED

Peace through war

1.30 a.m.

U.N. move for cease-fire

U.S. 'neutral' in conflict

Ruling the skies

Sabotage units

Reports say airports of 3 Arab Capitals strafed

FRENCH SAID HALTING AID TO ISRAEL

MESSAGE FROM TEDDY KOLLEK, MAYOR OF JERUSALEM

Eban: took arms in self-defence

Gov't House taken

Aid from Holland

NEW YORK STOCK EXCHANGE

Beit Hasefer Reali announces the death of **Dr. Arthur Biram**, founder and first principal of the school.

THE JERUSALEM

POST

FRIDAY, MARCH 2, 1973 • ADAR A 28, 5733 • MUHARRAM 27, 1393 • VOL. XLIII, No. 13731

NIXON TO GOLDA MEIR:

U.S. TO CONTINUE SUPPORTING ISRAEL

'Ready to meet Egypt' Discuss moves for peace

THE JERUSALEM

POST

60 PAGES (including 48-page magazine)

Iron Curtain Page 5

Price: IL1.50

FRIDAY, SEPTEMBER 14, 1973 • ELUL 17, 5733 • SHA'ABAN 16, 1393 • VOL. XLIII, No. 13894*

Thirteen Syrian Mig 21s downed

Israeli jet lost, pilot is rescued

THE JERUSALEM

POST

SECOND EDITION

Price: IL1.50

Israel drives 10 kms. towards Damascus

800 tanks destroyed, taken; Israeli planes blast targets

Three Arab terrorists die after butchering 20 in Galilee town

THE JERUSALEM

POST

Ma'alot stories pictures Pages 2, 3, 10

Price: 80 Ag.

THURSDAY, MAY 16, 1974 • IYAR 24, 5734 • RABI TANI 25, 1394 • VOL. XLII, No. 14006*

Day-long drama ends with sixteen children murdered in school house

Sign Number Nineteen

The Diaspora

That the Jews would be scattered into all nations is prophesied in the Old Testament from Genesis to Malachi. Moses even foretold in Deuteronomy 28 that those that were not killed would be sold on the Egyptian slave markets. Josephus records that this happened exactly as prophesied. The prophet Daniel even became ill when he was shown what would happen to his people during this period of worldwide dispersion. History proves that every detail prophesied about the Diaspora has been fulfilled.

The dispersion of Israel into all nations is not only prophesied in the Old Testament, it is prophesied also in the New Testament. Jesus Christ, within the context of the Olivet Discourse, foretold the persecution of Israel in all nations during the Diaspora: "And they shall fall by the edge of the sword, and shall be led away captive into all nations: and Jerusalem shall be trodden down of the Gentiles, until the times of the Gentiles be fulfilled" (Luke 21:24).

Every Old Testament prophet who prophesied the Diaspora also prophesied that it would end, and Jews out of all nations would return and the nation would live again. Jesus foretold the return in the parable of the fig tree; Peter and John foretold the return in Acts 15:14–17; Paul alluded to the return in Romans 11. The dispersion of Israel as foretold in the Bible has been proven by history. The return and refounding of Israel as a nation has been played out on a day-by-day basis before our very eyes as already noted in previous chapters in this book. The only remaining question to be considered is, when? When will the "times of the Gentiles" ultimately end? When will the Temple be rebuilt? When will the Messiah come to fulfill all of God's promises and covenants relating to Israel? While Jesus Christ said that no man could know the exact day or the hour, He referred us to signs given by Isaiah, Jeremiah, Daniel, the prophets, and Himself as indicators that "that day" was near, even at the door (Luke 21:31; Matthew 24:33).

A remarkable prophecy relating to the Diaspora and the return is found in Hosea 3:4–5; 4:1; 5:15; 6:1–2:

> For the children of Israel shall abide many days without a king, and without a prince, and without a sacrifice, and without an image, and without an ephod, and without teraphim:Afterward shall the children of Israel return, and seek the LORD their God, and David their king; and shall fear the LORD and his goodness in the latter days. . . . Hear the word of the LORD, ye children of Israel: for the LORD hath a controversy with the inhabitants of the land, because there is no truth, nor mercy, nor knowledge of God in the land. . . . I will go and return to my place, till they acknowledge their offence, and seek my face: in their affliction they will seek me early. . . . Come, and let us return unto the LORD: for he hath torn, and he will heal us; he hath smitten, and he will bind us up. After two days will he revive us: in the third day he will raise us up, and we shall live in his sight.

God revealed to the prophets that Israel would be scattered into all nations, but they were not told how long this period would be. Daniel pleaded with the Lord to tell him how long it would be before Israel received its full promised inheritance. This question also evidently troubled Hosea.

The explanation given by most pre-millennial Christian scholars is that the preceding prophecy by Hosea is to occur between the first advent and the second advent of Jesus Christ. The beginning of the Diaspora certainly corresponds with the prophecy of Jesus in that the starting point would be the destruction of Jerusalem and the Temple. Hosea was given a time period of two days for the duration of the Diaspora. Common sense would tell us that the Jews could not be scattered into all the world and then brought back in two twenty-four–hour days. We read in Psalm chapter ninety and Second Peter chapter three that one day is with the Lord as a thousand years. Although we cannot interpret this to mean that in every place in Scripture a day is to be understood as a thousand years, within the Diaspora setting it does have a literal application. The Diaspora has lasted for approximately two thousand years. Does this mean that Israel's Messiah will appear

At sundown on Shabbat the young Orthodox Jews gather arm-in-arm to march down to the Western Wall in celebration of the entrance of Shabbat

in the year 2000? Or, does this mean that Jesus Christ will return in the year 2000? I do not know, but I do believe it is another sign that His coming is near.

Dr. Kenneth Wuest, in his commentary on Galatians 4:4, interpreted this scripture to mean that there was a year, a month, a day, an hour, a minute for Jesus to be born. While Jesus said that no man could know the date of His return, He said that God had indeed appointed a definite day. On the basis that God created all things in six days, and man was to work six days, a traditional Christian teaching is that this age will end in six thousand years, which would approximate the year A.D. 2000. Edward Gibbons in *The Decline and Fall of the Roman Empire,* chapter fifteen, insisted that early church records indicate that even those who sat at the feet of the apostles were taught that Jesus would come back in the year A.D. 2000.

More than one hundred years ago Bishop Russell of Scotland wrote:

> It must be acknowledged that the doctrine concerning it stretches back into antiquity so remote and obscure, that it is impossible to fix its origin. The tradition that the earth, as well as the moral and religious state of its inhabitants, were to undergo a great change at the end of six thousand years, has been detected in the writings of Pagans, Jews, and Christians. It is found in the most ancient of those commentaries of the Old Testament, which we owe to the learning of the rabbinical school; . . . this will nevertheless leave no room for doubt that the notion of the millennium preceded by several centuries the introduction of the Christian faith.

Another appraisal of the A.D. 2000 messianic or millennial age was offered by Daniel Taylor and H. L. Hastings:

> David Gregory, a learned mathematician and astronomer of Oxford, England, who died in 1710, says: "In the first verse of the first chapter of Genesis, the Hebrew letter Aleph, which in the Jewish arithematic stands for one thousand, is six times found. From hence the ancient Cabalists concluded that the world would last six thousand years. Because also God was six days about the creation, and a thousand years with him are but as one day; Psalm 90:4; 2 Peter 3:8, therefore after six days, that is six thousand years duration of the world, there shall be a seventh day, or millenary sabbath rest. This early tradition of the Jews was found in the Sibylline Oracles and in Hesiod.

In the Epistle of Barnabas (c. 100–138) the proposition that this age will end in A.D. 2000 and a new age will begin, wherein the heavens will be refashioned, is repeatedly supported. And, we could continue and quote many traditional rabbinical and Christian sources that uphold the A.D. 2000 messianic theory. Another verse from Hosea would seem to also support or enforce the preceding thought:

> Then shall we know, if we follow on to know the LORD: his going forth is prepared as the morning; and he shall come unto us as the rain, as the latter and former rain unto the earth.
>
> —Hosea 6:3

This promise that follows immediately the healing of Israel after two days infers that the messianic age will appear when both the latter and former rains have been restored in Israel. The return of the rains has happened since Israel became a nation in 1948; therefore, the reasonable sequence is the coming of the Lord to bless Israel and bring in the millennial age.

Nevertheless, we could cite hundreds of false prophets who have set dates for the Lord's coming and been proven wrong. Christians should be ready for the coming of the Lord at any time—any minute of the day or night. And, of course, we are to pray for the peace of Jerusalem.

■ ■ ■ ■ ■

The Diaspora is, of course, a chapter in the history of the people of Israel. It is a stage in God's timetable—His plan and purpose for all things. According to the prophets, it was supposed to end at some point. There must also come a point where all the Israeli people, at least a majority, will live once more on the land of Israel.

Before World War II the world Jewish population was sixteen and a half million. At that time, only one-half million lived in the land of Israel, approximately three percent of the total Jewish world census. After World War II and the Holocaust, the world Jewish population was eleven and a half million, and six hundred fifty thousand lived in Israel, which was five and a half percent. Today, the world Jewish population is fourteen million, which includes five million Jews living in Israel, approximately forty percent. When the majority of the world Jewish population lives in Israel, that is when the "Year of Jubilee" will be observed again on the Jewish calendar. The fiftieth year of the refounding of Israel, which began on May 14, 1998, was a kind of Jubilee, but it was not the biblical Jubilee of sabbatical years. One day, we do not know when, a Jewish immigrant will come to make the majority. He will be greeted, perhaps at the Ben Gurion Airport in Tel Aviv. Perhaps bands will play and there will be a national celebration. The arrival of this one Jew, according to Jewish understanding, will bring the eschatological clock closer to the messianic age.

We are now witnessing the ingathering of the people of Israel back into the land of Israel. The rapid returning of Jews from all over the world back into the land is a very important sign of approaching messianic days.

Longfellow wrote a very beautiful poem called "The Jewish Cemetery in Rhode Island." He considers all the graves and names on the tombstones, and in his poem he wrote about all the wanderings and travails of the Jewish people. He ended the poem with the conclusion, "Dead nations never rise again." This may be true of nations like Assyria, but God never promised Assyria that it would rise again. However, God did promise through the prophets that Israel would indeed rise again. It is indeed miraculous to see and live in these times when God is fulfilling His promises, and we know that He will fulfill His promises and covenants regarding the future messianic Kingdom.

—Gilla

THE JERUSALEM POST

Vol. LIII, No. 15802 Friday, January 4, 1985 • Tevet 11, 5745 • Rabia Tani 11, 1405 IS500

Arrival in Israel seen as miracle by new olim • Absorption centres, hotels and army facilities mobilized to house thousands • Hospitals treat for malnutrition and unusual ailments • Newcomers, some barefoot, arrive without possessions

Wraps off massive operation to rescue Jews of Ethiopia

At top, a group of Ethiopian Jews a few hours after their "Magic Carpet" flight wait to be registered and get new clothing. At bottom, new arrivals shed sandals for tennis shoes. Many of the Ethiopian Jews arrived barefoot. (Louis Rapoport)

By JUDY SIEGEL and LOUIS RAPOPORT
Jerusalem Post Reporters

The official veil of secrecy on Israel's massive campaign to save the Jews of Ethiopia was lifted hurriedly yesterday, as government and Jewish Agency representatives told reporters in Jerusalem that "over 10,000" of them have arrived "in recent years."

A "press briefing on the absorption of Ethiopian immigrants" was held at Beit Agron, attended by local and foreign journalists. Officials disclosed some of the facts about the saving of Ethiopian Jews, which in the last two months has taken the form of a complex airlift, made more urgent by the recent drought and starvation in the African country.

The story of the rescue effort until now had been embargoed by voluntary agreement between the government and the Israel Editors' Committee so as not to jeopardize the operation. Only after news of the rescue dribbled out in the foreign and local press, and then became a flood in recent days, did authorities feel they had to make an official announcement.

The arrival of the immigrants – who come from an underdeveloped agrarian society and who arrive with their tattered rags as their only possessions – comes at a time of economic crisis. The estimated cost of the absorption of the Ethiopian Jews during the next two years is $300 million, some of which will be funded by the Jewish people abroad and some by U.S. refugee aid money.

The plan to rescue the most recent batch of Ethiopian Jews was taken by the Begin government and re-approved by the current government.

Yisrael Peleg, director of the Government Press Office, started the briefing by declaring that the Prime Minister's Office had asked the press office to provide reporters with details on the absorption of Ethiopian Jews. With him were acting Jewish Agency Executive chairman and permanent treasurer Akiva Lewinsky; Health Ministry Director-General Dan Michaeli; Deputy Director-General of the Absorption Ministry Shmuel Shenhar; and Moshe Gilboa, director of the World Jewish Affairs Division of the Foreign Ministry.

Lewinsky, filling in for executive chairman Arye Dulzin who is abroad on Agency business, said that "everyone in Israel feels the presence of Ethiopian Jews in the country." The big drama, he added, is their future absorption into Israeli society. "One day, a great deal will be written." Because of the Ethiopian Jews' background, their absorption will be much more diffi-

Related story — Page 3

cult than those who came from the West, said Lewinsky. Aware of this, the interministerial committee, coordinated by the Absorption Ministry, which has directed the various authorities was determined "not to repeat mistakes" committed years ago with other groups of immigrants.

A total of 1,500 Ethiopian children have been placed in Youth Aliya institutions – all of them religiously oriented because of the observant nature of the Ethiopian Jewish community.

Michaeli disclosed that 300 of the immigrants are now in local hospitals. Doctors have accumulated considerable experience in treating the unusual diseases and problems suffered by the Ethiopian Jews. He emphasized that there is no danger to the public from these ailments, and that modern treatment of malaria, tuberculosis and parasitic diseases are quicker and more efficient than in the past.

The newcomers, presented with immigrants' certificates on their arrival, are examined by medical specialists and those not requiring immediate treatment are sent to absorption centres and other facilities around the country.

(Continued on Page 14)

Premature publication

By JUDY SIEGEL
Jerusalem Post Reporter

Press leaks about the Ethiopian rescue forced the authorities to acknowledge the "open secret" yesterday rather than to present the whole saga after the operation was ended, as they had planned to do.

Yesterday's disclosure was precipitated by an interview with Yehuda Dominitz, director-general of the Jewish Agency's aliya department. front pages. As a result, the Associated Press picked up the story, embellishing it with reports that it had obtained from abroad. More international news agencies and Israel Radio followed.

It was officially announced that Dominitz had been told by Aharon, who is in London for Agency meetings, to "go on vacation." Domi-

(Continued on Page 3, Col. 4)

Israel takes offensive, bitter battles raging

Port Said military targets bombed

Jerusalem Post Arab Affairs Reporter

The Egyptians said last night that Port Said at the Mediterranean end of the Suez Canal was bombarded. The Cairo military command said this was the first time an Egyptian city had been bombarded, and warned that Israel "will have to bear the consequences of this operation."

Cairo Radio claimed that a number of houses and buildings were set on fire.

The Israel Army spokesman said last night that the Air Force went into action last night against military installations in the Port Said area.

Egypt's Foreign Minister, Mohammed Hassan Zayyat, interrupted the U.N. General Assembly's debate last night to charge that Port Said had been bombarded.

AFTER MIDNIGHT

An Egyptian De Castro-type minesweeper was hit by an Israel Navy vessel in the Gulf of Suez yesterday and went up in flames. The army spokesman said late last night that none of the Israeli vessels which participated in the battle was hit.

* * *

The spokesman said Israel planes during the day attacked missile batteries and other military installations in the Port Said region, rendering the batteries inoperative and badly damaging the installations.

Skyhawk jet screeches overhead as Israeli troops move up road in Golan Heights to join in yesterday's counter-offensive against the Syrians.

THE JERUSALEM POST

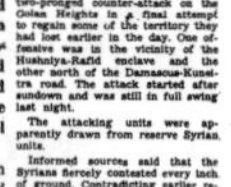

Price: 65 Ag.

TUESDAY, OCTOBER 9, 1973 • TISHRE 13, 5734 • RAMADHAN 13, 1393 • VOL. XLIII, No. 13912*

SYRIAN ARMOURED UNITS BID TO COUNTER-ATTACK

By ZEEV SCHUL and BONNIE HOPE, Post Military Reporters

TEL AVIV. — The Chief of Staff, Rav-Aluf David Elazar, last night confirmed that the tides of war had turned: that the Israel Defence Forces were now on the offensive on all fronts and that they "would continue to attack and destroy the enemy wherever and whenever he can be found..." Speaking to foreign and local military correspondents at Beit Sokolow, the Chief of Staff indicated that the army would not feel itself bound by any existing boundaries.

"The cease-fire line is not marked on the terrain where the fighting is taking place. We are now engaged in battle in that area and will fight wherever necessary in order to destroy the enemy." In reply to an earlier question as to whether he could confirm that Israeli troops had crossed the Suez Canal in pursuit of the Egyptians, the Chief of Staff replied with a laconic, "Not yet."

In his opening statement, the Chief of Staff lauded the outstanding fighting qualities of Israel's regular army which, he said, had blunted the advance of the two enemy armies. "All units fought in an exemplary manner. I think that the soldiers of 1973 are even better than those of 1967, who were better than those of 1956, who were better than those of 1948..." He added that reporters would yet "sing the praises of their exploits for a long time to come..."

R/A Elazar said that he could not, for the time being, disclose the number of Israeli casualties. "The quicker we advance and the stronger we attack, the fewer casualties we will suffer and the more the enemy will suffer."

Asked about the positions of the forces, the Chief of Staff remarked that fighting was still in progress. But he said that the Syrians had been completely ousted from the sector north of Kuneitra in the Golan. In the Hushniya region in central Golan, where the Syrians had made what he termed as a "very deep penetration," Israel had destroyed part of the invading force and ousted most of the others "although a few units may be a few hundred metres inside our lines." The same applied to the southern sector of the Heights where some Syrian units were still in the Rafid enclave region.

As to the Suez Canal, the Egyptians still held three bridgeheads (minus bridges) but are surrounded and they have retreated from some of the areas held by them earlier.

TO HIT OUT

General Elazar would not go into any details concerning operational plans but said: "Our aim is to hit out at the enemy — to cause them as many casualties as possible — to teach them a lesson and to win a decisive and significant victory — in short, to break all their bones."

Queried on an explanation for the belated mobilization orders given to reservists, the Chief of Staff remarked that the Premier and the Defence Minister had already explained the dominant considerations. But he stressed that the attack had not come as a surprise and that the frontline forces had been ready and braced for the onslaught and did everything within their means when it came.

Asked to compare the Arab and Israeli armies, the Chief of Staff remarked that the Arabs had more modern, better, and larger quantities of armour and other weapons than they had before. "But under actual battle conditions it was the Arabs who broke and were defeated, showing that the quality gap between the soldiers of the Israeli and Arab armies remained as wide as ever."

R/A Elazar said that "many hundreds" of Egyptian and Syrian tanks had been destroyed. He said he could not give the exact figure.

A foreign correspondent mentioned a remark attributed to R/A Yitzhak Rabin that he had "forgotten" to capture the triangle on the east bank of the canal north of Kantara, extending to Port Fuad. Elazar raised a laugh when he said he would ask Rabin what he had forgotten and would try to put it right.

Another correspondent mentioned that the press has begun calling the current hostilities the "Yom Kippur War" and asked the Chief of Staff what he would call it. His reply: "The War of the Day of Judgement."

Jerusalem Post Military Correspondents

TEL AVIV. — Syrian armoured units late last night attempted a two-pronged counter-attack on the Golan Heights in a final attempt to regain some of the territory they had lost earlier in the day. One offensive was in the vicinity of the Hushniya-Rafid enclave and the other north of the Damascus-Kuneitra road. The attack started after sundown and was still in full swing last night.

The attacking units were apparently drawn from reserve Syrian units.

Informed sources said that the Syrians fiercely contested every inch of ground. Contradicting earlier reports, these sources said their armoured columns retreated in an orderly manner.

The Syrians lost tens of more aircraft yesterday, most of them in aerial combat. This number includes three new types of planes termed as Sukhoi 20's. The plane is claimed to be of a variable wing class but appears to be so new that it is not yet listed in the authoritative Observer's Book of Aircraft (1973 edition).

In the south, a three-pronged attack against the Egyptian spearheads included one IDF column sweeping on the road to Kantara, a second column on the Ismailiya-Bir Gafgafa axis and a third heading westwards to block the Mitla and Jidi passes.

While the Egyptians did not succeed in rebuilding their bridges, they are now operating a shuttle raft service across the waterway. Their dogged determination is shown by their continued shipment of reinforcements to the east bank of the Canal — and this in spite of having lost, like the Syrians, hundreds of tanks in battle during the course of the past three days.

Senior army officers stressed last night that in spite of favourable developments the Israel units still had a hard task ahead of them. More heavy fighting is expected today.

The Egyptians lost tens of planes yesterday, some of them in a second attempt to bomb the advancing Israeli columns.

Yariv adviser to Elazar

Aluf Aharon Yariv (Res.), the former Army Intelligence chief, has been appointed special adviser to the Chief of Staff.

Urgent messages now can reach soldiers

Civilians may now send urgent messages to members of their families serving in the armed forces — concerning births, weddings, britot mila and sickness — by dialling one of the following numbers: Jerusalem: 63111; Tel Aviv: 254122; and Haifa: 660961.

These numbers may be called, starting today, from 8 a.m. to 10 p.m. The service was made possible through the cooperation of the Civil Service Commission, the Ministry of Communications and the Army Radio.

Nixon to Brezhnev: Restore the peace

By DANIEL GOTTLIEB
Jerusalem Post Correspondent and Agencies

WASHINGTON. — President Nixon has appealed to Soviet Communist Party chief Leonid Brezhnev to join in a concerted big-power effort to restore peace to the Middle East, the White House disclosed yesterday. But presidential spokesman Ronald Ziegler would not reveal details of Mr. Nixon's message or of Mr. Brezhnev's response to the appeal made over the weekend.

Mr. Nixon told reporters the U.S. was seeking support for a position "which we hope and believe will be effective in stopping the fighting."

The White House declined to discuss Mr. Nixon's personal message to Mr. Brezhnev or the Soviet Party chief's response, which was received last night.

The President's appeal to Mr. Brezhnev was apparently an attempt to reach some measure of agreement with the Soviet Union in advance of the U.N. Security Council meeting.

Mr. Ziegler said the U.S. sought broad support from nations involved in the war and those with interests in the area to back Security Council efforts to halt the fighting.

Dr. Kissinger has kept in close touch with the Soviet Ambassador in Washington, Anatoly Dobrynin, and also consulted Israel and Egyptian diplomats, the White House said.

President Nixon, explaining to reporters the U.S. decision to take the Middle East crisis to the United Nations, said he had in mind "the importance of getting strong support for the position the United States will take."

At the State Department, spokesman Robert McCloskey told reporters the U.S. had not urged Israel to stop short of crossing the 1967 cease-fire line, although it had urged restraint on all parties to the fighting.

Mr. McCloskey said it was unfair to speculate that the U.S. did not want an immediate cease-fire in order to give Israel time to regain lost ground.

Informed sources said yesterday that Israel does not expect the U.S. to press for a cease-fire before Arab forces are pushed back to the 1967 cease-fire lines. This is regarded as the U.S. side of a secret understanding struck between Washington and Jerusalem. Israel, for its part, kept its side of the "agreement" by not launching pre-emptive strikes when it learnt that Arab forces were massing.

The U.S. is walking a tightrope in its handling of the latest Middle East crisis in order not to antagonize the Arabs. President Nixon's statement, explaining the U.S. call for yesterday's Security Council session, was significant in its vagueness.

"We are developing support for a position which we hope and believe will be effective in stopping the fighting," the President told reporters called into his office as he met with Secretary of State Henry Kissinger.

Israel would like the U.S. to hold off any cease-fire resolution in the U.N. for another 72 hours, the time it believes required for expelling the Egyptians from the east bank of the Canal and the Syrians from the Golan Heights line.

(See Brezhnev — page 2)

Israel seen attacking across cease-fire lines

By ASHER WALLFISH and DAVID LANDAU
Jerusalem Post Reporters

Israel is expected to extend the army's counter-attack into a full-blown punitive offensive across the cease-fire lines against the Egyptian and Syrian invaders. At the outset of the war, the decision in principle was taken to smash the enemy's armed might. Now, the military position on the ground and international political situation enable Israel to move from counter-attack to all-out offensive action.

Some foreign diplomats in Tel Aviv told The Post that Israel enjoyed "a reserve of sympathy" at the present stage of the conflict. The incontestable proof that Israel was the victim of premeditated aggression, and the consequent damage which it suffered, made it seem reasonable for Israeli forces to cross the cease-fire lines in hot pursuit of Syrian and Egyptian forces. As long as Israel did not occupy further territory, it need not lose this sympathy, the diplomats believed.

The Cabinet met at nine last night to hear reports from the battlefields and from the political arena at New York, where the Security Council was to convene.

There have been no approaches to Israel from any state to do anything or refrain from anything, one well-placed source told *The Jerusalem Post* in the early evening.

Constant contacts were being maintained with the U.S. But sources here were reluctant to divulge anything of their content.

"Our hands are not tied at this stage," the source told *The Post*. "I think they (the Arabs) must be made to pay the price. We must hit them very hard for the dirty trick they pulled on us..."

At any rate, the source continued, Israel's immediate considerations at this stage were strategic, not political.

After the Cabinet meeting last night the following communique was issued:

"At the Cabinet's second meeting yesterday, the Chief of Staff reported on the situation on the war fronts.

The Minister of Finance reported on problems of financing the war effort and on the mobilization of the Jews of the world, especially in the U.S., Canada, Europe, Australia and South Africa.

He also reported on his meetings — to discuss the war effort — with the Histadrut Central Committee, the Manufacturers Association, the bank managers, the insurance companies, the Citrus Marketing Board and the artisans' representatives.

The Ministerial Economic Committee will meet today for a detailed discussion of the issue."

U.N. urges return to previous positions

UNITED NATIONS. — U.N. Ambassador John Scali told the Security Council after midnight last night that the U.S. wants the two sides to return to their positions which they held before the Middle East war broke out on Saturday.

He made the statement after the Council met following a postponement without explanation from a scheduled earlier meeting.

Shortly before the announcement of the postponement, U.S. Ambassador John Scali, who requested the special session, held intense private consultations with other key delegates.

Informed sources said they were trying to work out an agreed resolution calling for a cease-fire, but that disagreements which marked similar private talks over the weekend still persisted.

The informants said the U.S. favoured a cease-fire with withdrawal of Egyptian and Syrian troops to the October 5 lines along the Suez Canal and in the Golan Heights.

The Western European members — France, Britain and Austria — were said to want a simple cease-fire resolution with a provision that this should not prejudice the lines to be drawn between the opposing forces.

African and Asian members of the Council were reported to be ready to propose a cease-fire coupled with a call for Israeli forces to be withdrawn to the pre-June, 1967, lines.

EBAN TELLS U.N. ASSEMBLY:

'Secure borders saved Israel'

UNITED NATIONS. — Israeli Foreign Minister Abba Eban told the General Assembly yesterday that if Israel had performed "the folly" of going back to the previous armistice lines, then it might have been destroyed by the latest Arab attacks.

Mr. Eban told the Assembly, which interrupted its general debate to hear statements on the war situation, that the Arab aggression proved Israel's insistence on "precise" negotiations for a peace settlement.

Egyptian Foreign Minister Mohamed Zayyat charged that Israel had launched a "decoy attack," and Egypt acted in self-defence. Zayyat took the floor after Syrian Foreign Minister Ismail Zakaria made the opening statement, accusing Israel of launching the aggression against his country and Egypt.

Mr. Eban said Israel had suffered a "tragic loss of life and blood." But he said Egypt and Syria have suffered much more "as a result of their leader's cynical aggression." He charged their attacks will go down in history "as one of the basest acts of which a government can have been responsible."

"There is not a single man or woman inside or outside of this hall who doesn't know in his heart" that Egypt and Syria started the war.

Mr. Eban said he had a telegram from Israel last Saturday, six hours before hostilities began, saying that an attack was coming from the Arabs.

Having been forewarned, he said, Israel communicated assurances to the Arabs — presumably through a third party — that it would not take pre-emptive action.

He said the Arabs "invented the myth" of a ship crossing the Suez Canal silently in the darkness early on Yom Kippur.

"How idiotic would a man have to be to believe that on a day when there are no communications, with the vast majority of our soldiers in their homes or synagogues, when even forward posts are manned at their minimum level, that precisely on this day Israel would launch a war — on the day holiest to all those who cherish Jewish solidarities, in order to invite thousands of Egyptian and Syrian tanks to attack across a relatively undefended and totally quiescent line."

"The inconceivable mendacity of this allegation is fully exposed by the military facts and by the re-

(Continued on page 5, col. 3)

BAR OF GOLD

PARIS (UPI). — A Frenchman walked into the Israel Embassy yesterday, laid a bar of gold on a table and said, "I want to give this to you." Embassy officials said they have not decided yet what to do with the gold, worth 14,000 francs (about IL14,000).

3 Syrian Sukhois fall near Metulla

Jerusalem Post Reporter

METULLA. — Residents here yesterday watched three Syrian Sukhoi bombers crash in flames just to the south of their settlement after a brief dog-fight with Israeli jets.

The three Syrian planes came from the direction of Lebanon, one of the eyewitnesses told *The Post*, apparently intending to bomb Kiryat Shmona. Israeli fighters suddenly appeared overhead. They engaged the Syrian jets and, after a brief dog-fight lasting no more than a few seconds, three loud explosions were heard and the Sukhois fell in flames.

Showers start in the south

Heavy showers fell yesterday about 15 minutes in the southern coastal plain, from Khan Yunis to Rafah. Scattered drops also fell in other parts of central and southern Israel.

The weatherman said last night that the unusually low temperatures for this time of year would continue today.

Kantara 'residents' greet Egyptians

Jerusalem Post Arab Affairs Reporter

Egypt last night claimed it recaptured the ghost town of Kantara, east of the Suez Canal, alleging that the population in the completely deserted place have come out "in their masses" to greet the advancing Egyptian forces.

The Egyptians said they hoisted their flag over the town, and said "the Sinai district administration will be reinstated soon in Kantara," the region's former provincial capital.

The military communique said Egyptian troops had fought from street to street and building to building to force the Israeli occupying force to surrender. It said Egyptian forces had captured 30 Israelis "the only Israelis who survived in the city."

"The Egyptians still in the city were overjoyed and rushed to welcome brother Egyptians fighting for the honour of their country," the communique added.

The Egyptian claim was contained in "military communique number 16," which was the third issued yesterday. The previous two communiques, which came after 13 hours of silence, claimed the Egyptians were "in full control of the entire east bank of the Suez Canal," and said they were advancing deep into Sinai.

The Egyptian and Syrian claims of success came in the face of the decisive Israeli push.

The Syrians yesterday claimed they inflicted heavy losses to Israel's Air Force after constant air battles. The Syrians also claimed control of most of the central region in the Golan Heights, and said they were advancing deeper into the area.

The Cairo and the Damascus statements were made as their forces were hit by the Israeli counter-attack, which ended the Egyptian and Syrian offensives at mid-morning yesterday.

In a late communique, the Cairo military command claimed that Egyptian forces have carried out successful operations to deny Israel the use of oil wells at Bala'een on the western coast of Sinai. The Egyptians said that their forces raided the oil wells and left them in flames after clashing with Israeli troops and returning to their base "safely."

Other reports from Cairo said the Egyptian government ordered new emergency regulations, including rationing petrol for civilians and

(Continued on page 2, col. 4)

Sirens in Haifa

HAIFA. — Air raid sirens ordered Haifa residents into their bomb shelters twice yesterday morning. No reason was given for the alerts, which occurred around 9 and 10 a.m. The all-clear was sounded 10 minutes after the first alert and 50 minutes after the second. (Itim)

Sign Number Twenty

Restoration of Temple Worship

The Tabernacle served as a place of communication, worship, and sacrifice with God for Israel during the period of wandering in the wilderness and the time of the judges. King David envisioned a permanent Temple to replace the Tabernacle (2 Samuel 7:1–2; 1 Kings 7:18). Because David was a man of war, he was not permitted to build the Temple, but he did purchase a site for it from Araunah, the Jebusite. The Temple was constructed by Solomon and dedicated as the "house of the Lord God" (2 Chronicles 3:1).

Solomon's Temple stood for four hundred sixteen years

Model of Temple

before it was plundered and burned by the Babylonians in 586 B.C. on the ninth day of Av. After the Babylonian captivity period ended, a returning Jewish remnant under the leadership of Zerubbabel completed the rebuilding of the Temple in 515 B.C. Because Zerubabbel did not have the funds and skilled workmen available to him as Solomon did, the second Temple was inferior in beauty and workmanship. However, Zerubbabel's Temple was refurbished and enlarged by King Herod. The second Temple was burned by the Romans on the ninth day of Av in A.D. 70.

There is a difference of opinion among Orthodox and/or observing Jews whether the Temple must be rebuilt before the Messiah comes. Chapters forty through forty-four of Ezekiel relate to the building of the Millennial Temple, or Messianic Temple, so there will be such a Temple. The prophet Zechariah foretold that the Messiah will build this Temple:

> . . . Behold the man whose name is The BRANCH; and he shall grow up out of his place, and he shall build the temple of the LORD: Even he shall build the temple of the LORD; and he shall bear the glory, and shall sit and rule upon his throne; and he shall be a priest upon his throne: and the counsel of peace shall be between them both.
>
> —Zechariah 6:12–13

According to Malachi 3:1, the Lord of the covenant with Israel will suddenly come to His Temple. Jesus proposed that He was not only "the branch," He was the vine (John 15:5). Jesus also suddenly came to the Temple and in rage threw out the money changers. He also, according to the Gospels, made the blind to see, the deaf to hear, and the lame to leap as a deer. He fulfilled these promised messianic miracles in type according to Paul in order to prove His claim to Israel as the

Messiah: "Now I say that Jesus Christ was a minister of the circumcision for the truth of God, to confirm the promises made unto the fathers" (Romans 15:8).

We present this basic foundation information to present the evidence that Jesus Christ never confirmed a covenant with Israel. Some in Israel did believe that He was the Christ, but most did not. Jesus was rejected. This leaves us with the proposition that a false messiah must come and confirm the covenant with Israel, and after three and a half years repudiate his confirmation and stop the sacrifice and oblation:

> And he shall confirm the covenant with many for one week: and in the midst of the week he shall cause the sacrifice and the oblation to cease, and for the overspreading of abominations he shall make it desolate, even until the consummation, and that determined shall be poured upon the desolate.
>
> —Daniel 9:27

The pronoun "it" is in italics, meaning that this evil person will simply make desolations on earth.

> And arms shall stand on his part, and they shall pollute the sanctuary of strength, and shall take away the daily sacrifice, and they shall place the abomination that maketh desolate.
>
> —Daniel 11:31

> And from the time that the daily sacrifice shall be taken away, and the abomination that maketh desolate set up, there shall be a thousand two hundred and ninety days.
>
> —Daniel 12:11

> When ye therefore shall see the abomination of desolation, spoken of by Daniel the prophet, stand in the holy place, (whoso readeth, let him understand:).
>
> —Matthew 24:15

> Let no man deceive you by any means: for that day shall not come, except there come a falling away first, and that man of sin be revealed, the son of perdition; Who opposeth and exalteth himself above all that is called God, or that is worshipped; so that he as God sitteth in the temple of God, shewing himself that he is God.
>
> —2 Thessalonians 2:3–4

Considering every prophecy relating to the "abomination of desolation" in the Temple, this awful sin will be enacted at the halfway mark of the Tribulation in a temple structure on the Temple Mount. The act constitutes a satanically possessed dictator who stands in the Temple declaring to the entire world that he is the Messiah (Christ), and demanding that all nations worship him as God (Revelation 13). A period of international desolation descriptive of nuclear warfare ensues. Related scriptures foretell the destruction of Damascus, Iraq, and many other nations, including Egypt, being so contaminated that no animal can live on the land for forty years. Many other world desolations are prophesied for this time in the book of Revelation.

Some have suggested that a tabernacle could be placed in front of the Western Wall to fulfill this prophecy, but in Amos 9:14 and Acts 15:16 where the tabernacle is mentioned, the Messiah in Amos, and Jesus Christ in Acts, are indicated as builders of the tabernacle. Therefore, the tabernacle in these scriptures seems to refer to the Davidic throne and theocratic government, not a literal structure.

However, evidence would substantiate the conclusion that there must be a Temple on the Temple Mount for the false messiah, or the Antichrist, to desecrate. This building doubtless will be destroyed, possibly at the battle of Armageddon. Nevertheless, there is increasing sentiment in Israel today to go ahead and make preparations for rebuilding the Temple, even though Moslem guards are still in control of the Temple Mount. The Temple Institute in Jerusalem is preparing the vessels needed in Temple worship, and the trumpets to welcome the Messiah. Cohens and Levites are being schooled to resume Temple worship, and many observing Jews have been excited about the appearance of a red heifer that would fulfill requirements in Numbers 19 for resuming Temple services. Most Orthodox and oberving Jews believe that the nation of Israel cannot be completely restored until the Temple, the Lord's House, is once more standing on Mount Moriah. This is certainly one of the more important messianic signs in Israel today.

▪ ▪ ▪ ▪ ▪

Jewish people understand somewhat differently; but, nevertheless, we do believe that the Temple must be rebuilt in order for messianic days to come. It is not entirely clear to many if the Temple will be rebuilt first, or if Messiah will come first, or the if two will coincide. It is generally believed, however, that the Temple will be rebuilt first. There are many evident signs that this may happen. The Temple Institute is not only in the process of remaking Temple vessels, musical instruments, and furnishings, but they are also doing research about the Temple, teaching about the Temple, and employing expert craftsmen in making the vessels for worship services. The Temple Institute already has trumpets, the vessels for the blood sacri-

fices, the menorah, the lots to cast on the Day of Atonement, and many other things that will be necessary when the Temple is rebuilt. This organization is certainly making all the needed preparations for the rebuilding of the Temple and Temple worship. Of course, the vessels are made according to biblical specifications, and some of them are very costly, as gold and silver is required as necessary metals.

There are other yeshivas *in the Old City training Cohens (priests) and Levites in the order and ecclesiastics of resuming Temple worship. Should the Temple be ready today, the priests and Levite attendants would be ready. It is fascinating how all these things have been retained in the Jews' knowledge down through many generations. Descendants of Aaron are called Cohens, but one Cohen, a doctor in Baltimore, Maryland, was interested to know if the Cohens today are actually descendants of Aaron. Of course, this information is recorded in the birth certificates of Cohens and Levites, but he wanted to check and prove for himself. So this doctor took some genetic material (DNA) from the inner cheek of men of the priestly families from all over the world—from Yemen, from Asia, from Europe, from the U.S., and from all over the world. Of course, humans have forty-six chromosomes—forty-four autosomes and two sex chromosomes. Men have* XY *sex chromosomes, and women have* XX *sex chromosomes. It was discovered that in the* Y *chromosome of the Cohens, regardless of the color of their skin, there was this little variation that was common in all, which indicated they had to have a common ancestor, and without doubt this ancestor was Aaron. The tribal separation and biblical rules concerning marriage had been maintained so strictly, that they all have this genetic feature. We can be sure they are qualified to resume Temple worship when the Temple is rebuilt.*

There was a Professor Koestler, author of The Thirteenth

Tribe, *who proposed that most of the Jews in Israel today, especially the Ashkenazi Jews, were Kazars who lived in the Caspian Sea area of Russia. Supposedly, according to Koestler, these Kazars converted to Judaism and migrated to Eastern Europe, so most of the Euroean Jews must not be Jews by race, and these are the majority of Jews in Israel today. This certainly is not historically correct, and the DNA tests I have referred to would also disprove this untenable theory.*

All these factors in Israel today relating to the rebuilding of the Temple and the resumption of Temple worship are graphic messianic signs of the coming age in which Israel will receive the covenant promises of the Lord.

—Gilla

Israel, Egypt sign truce accord

ACCORD SIGNED — Scene inside tent at Kilometre 101 of the Cairo-Suez road where the Israeli-Egyptian cease-fire agreement was signed yesterday. Israeli delegation on left shows Aluf Aharon Yariv, in dark glasses, who signed for Israel with his aides sitting beside him. At top of U-shaped table is UNEF commander, Finnish General Ensio Siilasvuo, flanked by two aides. Opposite Israelis are the Egyptians, with Egyptian Major-General Mohammed Gamazy who signed, at extreme left, sitting opposite Aluf Yariv. (David Rubinger)

Both sides 'correct' at brief ceremony

By CHARLES WEISS, Jerusalem Post Reporter

The American-inspired, six-point cease-fire agreement was signed by Egyptian and Israeli officers yesterday in a drab army tent pitched in the desert at Kilometre 101 on the Cairo-Suez road.

The principals arrived promptly at 3 p.m. They exchanged salutes — not handshakes — with each other. The Israeli delegation of six sat on the east side of the tent opposite the four Egyptians. At the head table sat three UN officers.

The Israelis were were led by Aluf Aharon Yariv and the Egyptians by General Mohammed Gamazy. The UNEF commander, General Ensio Siilasvuo, sat at the head table, and called the proceedings to order. He said: "Gentlemen, let's sign," according to the spokesman of the UNEF, who came from Cairo for the ceremony.

He said it took place just a few minutes after the men took their seats. Each side signed three copies in English, handed them over to the others, and then signed their three. He described the mood in the tent as "correct."

Once signatures were affixed, the flaps of the tent were raised, and the several hundred journalists crowded behind barbed wire fences put up about 25 metres away on both sides — Egyptian and Israeli — could see, vaguely, what was going on.

Photographers and journalists were then given 35 minutes to peek inside from closer up. The generals glumly posed for pictures.

Then the press was shooed away and both sides settled down to work on details for putting the agreement into effect. After about half-an-hour, the officers took a ten-minute break. No details at all were released of these talks.

But in a statement made during the intermission, Aluf Yariv said that the agreement was the "first step on the long and difficult road that leads to settlement of the conflict and to peace."

(A United Nations spokesman in Cairo said last night that the second meeting between Egyptians and Israelis to discuss the implementation of the agreement would be held today at 10 a.m. again at kilometre 101.

(The spokesman, Rudolf Stadjuhar, said the two parties, after the signing, started discussion yesterday on modalities of the implementation of the agreement. He described the talks that followed the signing of the agreement as "useful and constructive." Today's meeting will be attended by Gen. Gamazy and Aluf Yariv.)

It was learned later that the talks went on for several hours as the two sides tried to hammer out an acceptable interpretation of the text they had signed.

Most of the excitement and drama was provided by the press itself. Newsmen who came from Egypt broke ranks first. At one point, they tried to push their way by sheer muscle through the ranks of Egyptian military police and U.N. guards standing with fixed bayonets. That didn't work, and they were allowed close up by ones and twos.

Then the Israel-based newspapermen tried. Groups of six were permitted through the military police but the problem was in deciding which six. Everyone wanted to be among the first, and there were more than a hundred.

It kicked up a lot of dust, raised a lot of tempers and even had an effect on the negotiations inside the tent. When the scuffling became really wild, with shouting and curses, several of the officers in the tent turned to see what all the trouble about.

A number of observers noted that the day was November 11, the 55th anniversary of the 1918 armistice that ended "the war to end all wars."

General Yariv and Gamazy were applauded by Israeli and Egyptian soldiers respectively as they approached. An Israeli soldier shouted to Aluf Yariv: "Don't give in on the prisoners of war!"

No move yet, to meet today

By ARI RATH, Jerusalem Post Reporter

The signing of the cease-fire agreement between Israel and Egypt yesterday did not go much beyond the actual ceremony: both sides were sticking to their different interpretations of the six-point accord.

As a result there was a delay in the setting up of the U.N. check point at kilometre 101 on the Cairo-Suez road. This move would have signified that the cease-fire agreement was actually taking effect on the ground, and that the first Israeli prisoners of war were to be returned.

It is understood that both Aluf Yariv and General Gamazy agreed to sign first and argue later, rather than delay the signing pending agreement on outstanding points.

A main issue is understood to be Egypt's insistence that the supply route to the town of Suez and to the beleaguered Third Army along the Cairo-Suez road be put under full U.N. control, a point to which Israel is firmly opposed.

U.S. Secretary of State Kissinger's written interpretation which was conveyed to the Israel government on Saturday from Peking, is understood to uphold the Israel understanding that the entire road is to remain under full Israel military control.

Talks between the Israel and Egyptian delegations on this and other points are to be resumed today.

First step to peace — Yariv

Here is the text of a prepared statement by Aluf Aharon Yariv, which he read out after signing the cease-fire agreement:

"By signing this agreement with Egypt, we have taken the first step on the long and difficult road that leads to a settlement of the conflict between us and our neighbours, and to peace with them.

"Let us not falter, let us not shy away. Let us see things as they are. Let us believe in our strength and put our trust in Zahal and the Jewish people in Israel and the Diaspora.

If there are doubts — if there is worry about our first step — let us say clearly that Zahal is standing fast and ready, and will remain standing fast and ready, to protect our interests on this front as on all other fronts.

"Zahal is our main insurance that we can proceed safely along the difficult road ahead of us."

BULLETIN

NICOSIA (UPI). — Two International Red Cross planes may fly to Tel Aviv and Cairo today to begin the first prisoner of war exchange between Israel and Egypt, a Red Cross spokesman said here last night.

Arabs want settlement in 4 weeks

Jerusalem Post Arab Affairs Reporter

The Egyptians expect their immediate outstanding problems with Israel to be settled within four weeks under the new truce agreement signed between the two sides yesterday. Egypt's government spokesman, Ahmed Anis, last night said that yesterday's accord was a "prelude" to a peace conference which the Cairo press expects to be held on the second week of December in Geneva.

Anis said that the agreement was the first move towards implementation of the U.N. Security Council Middle East resolutions aimed at settling the Israel-Arab conflict. He indicated that Egypt and Israel will now engage in intensive talks to solve immediate issues before the peace conference in which other Arab delegates will participate.

Anis stressed the question of Israel's withdrawal to the "October 22 cease-fire lines" as being one of the immediate outstanding issues. He made no mention of an exchange of prisoners. Anis said that yesterday's agreement was necessary in order "to determine the positions" especially on the western bank of the Suez Canal — where Israel has captured a bulge stretching from Ismailia to south of Suez. He said that the disengagement of the forces under the current truce would eventually lead to peace negotiations for the implementation of the Security Council resolutions "calling for an Israel withdrawal from all occupied Arab territories," which Israel captured in 1967.

Egyptian news media yesterday treated the truce agreement with evident scepticism. The Egyptian state radio networks and newspapers called for the maintenance of a high state of military preparedness.

Meanwhile, Beirut's "L'Orient Le Jour" yesterday claimed that Egypt has consolidated its military strength on the western bank of the Suez Canal by establishing a Fourth Army, which includes some 25,000 Algerian soldiers.

The paper attributed the report to a correspondent who accompanied Lebanon's Premier Takieddin Solh on his return home from a weekend visit to Cairo. The correspondent reported Solh as having quoted President Sadat as claiming that his armed forces, including the encircled Third Army, preserved their military strength "and would come out with surprises" should the fighting be renewed.

But Solh quoted Sadat as emphasizing that he was in favour of quick progress in the current peace efforts, although stressing that he had no intention of forming diplomatic relations with Israel. According to Solh, Sadat said that Security Council resolution 242 did not call upon Egypt to recognize Israel, but only its borders.

Seven incidents on both fronts

Jerusalem Post Military Correspondent

TEL AVIV. — A relatively quiet day was reported from the two fronts yesterday.

Five out of the total of seven incidents reported during the day took place along the Syrian lines — all of them in the Mazrat Beit Jann sector. At 7.50 a.m. there was a burst of machinegun fire directed at IDF outposts followed some two hours later by two salvoes of artillery fire. There were three more rounds at 11 a.m. and more machinegun fire bursts at noon and 2.10 p.m. IDF units did not return the fire.

In the south, a single shell was lobbed into the Israeli lines southeast of Mantara, at 11 a.m. A second incident occurred at 12.40 p.m. northeast of the Great Bitter Lake where a Third Army machinegunner fired a single burst into the Israeli lines. There were no casualties.

KLM refused ground service in Damascus

DAMASCUS (Reuter). — Damascus airport workers last night refused to provide ground services for a KLM Royal Dutch airlines plane because of Holland's alleged pro-Israeli attitude. The airliner which flew in from Beirut, returned to the Lebanese capital 40 minutes after landing.

Air transport workers said in a statement that the boycott was in accordance with resolutions voted by Syria's general workers federation and by a pan-Arab labour federation conference in Libya earlier this month. Under the conference resolutions, all Dutch and U.S. transport and goods were to be boycotted, the statement said.

Civilian air traffic here returned to normal only yesterday when the airport was reopened after being closed for 36 days because of the Middle East war.

Airport workers placed a large placard on the tarmac saying in French and English: "The air transport workers in Syria strongly condemn the imperialist-Zionist aggression against their Arab nation and condemn the American and Dutch aid to Israel."

THE JERUSALEM POST

SECOND EDITION

Price: 65 Ag.

MONDAY, NOVEMBER 12, 1973 • HESHVAN 17, 5734 • SHAWWAL 18, 1393 • VOL. XLIII, No. 13940*

ELAZAR SAYS ARMY'S PROBE TO BE 'UNFLINCHING'

Jerusalem Post Reporter

TEL AVIV. — The Chief of Staff, Rav-Aluf David Elazar, yesterday told newsmen the Israel Defence Forces would unflinchingly draw all the necessary conclusions from the internal army inquiry into reported shortcomings on the eve of the Yom Kippur War and the conduct of the war itself. He said the army inquiry, approved yesterday by the Cabinet, at his request, would in no way substitute for the investigation — by a legal or public body — planned by the Government.

The army would investigate four main areas: intelligence information and assessment on the eve of the war, the state of military preparedness when the war broke out, the actual conduct of the war, and fighting doctrines.

Rav-Aluf Elazar said that the entire army was put on full battle alert — the highest state of military preparedness by the regular army. A few hours later the first teams of reservists were called up, in preparation for the general mobilization.

At the same time, he was aware that there were some serious failures in observing the order for full battle alert at some of the lower echelons, the extent of which will have to be determined by the inquiry.

Had the reserves been called up 24 or 48 hours earlier, the war would undoubtedly have looked different and casualties would have been fewer, said R/A. Elazar. The decision not to call up the reserves was taken at the highest military-political level on the basis of an assessment that despite all the signs of Egyptian and Syrian mass troop concentrations, there would be no war at that stage.

"We will never know whether the war would have broken out, had we called up the reserves, a move that might have caused the enemy to put off the attack for some time. But then we could have had a war a couple of weeks later, soon after the reserves were released," he said.

"This is in the very nature of things when a small regular army of a small nation has to face two huge regular armies, such as those of Egypt and Syria," he explained. "Although there is no hermetic defence, the chief task of the regular forces is to contain the enemy and then hit back and push back the enemy once the reserves move in, which is what actually happened in the October war," he said.

He realised there were some shortcomings in the way reserve units were equipped when they moved into the battle. But there were two sides to be heard on this point.

R/A Elazar said the alert of the Israel Defence Forces began 10 days before the war and reached its peak on Friday morning, as far as the regular army was concerned.

He recalled that last May the army had even more convincing intelligence data of stepped-up war preparations by the enemy. The government approved the assessment of the Chief of Staff and as a result some IL45m. were spent last May and June, in addition to the planned budget, to bolster the army's battle alert. In the event, war did not break out then.

The Chief of Staff took issue with "military experts" who seek to analyse the war in the press, exaggerating the significance of unimportant details. "It is a well-known fact that the individual commander cannot see the full picture of the battle and is concerned chiefly with his section of the front. But the final outcome of the battle is the result of the joint effort by different units and contingents. It may be less glamorous to fight for the holding of a bridgehead, rather than driving your tanks into Africa, but the holding of the bridgehead may be the crucial move of a particular battle," he said.

He cautioned against drawing hasty conclusions in connection with various phases of the war before a thorough investigation had been carried out.

NOT SURPRISED

There was also the enormous quantity of Egyptian troops — between 70,000 to 80,000 men in seven divisions, five infantry and two armoured — that attacked in the first wave.

Another surprise was the quantity of anti-tank personal missiles which the Egyptians used at fairly close range. But there was no question that both the Egyptian and Syrian soldier this time showed far more motivation, self-sacrifice and efficiency than in previous wars.

Even brigade commanders learned of the war only the day it broke out. Lower-ranking officers were told only at the outbreak of the fighting that this time it was the real thing.

(See also page 2)

Cabinet to discuss war inquiry

Jerusalem Post Reporter

The Cabinet is to discuss "the question of the investigation and examination of issues connected with the war which need investigation," an official communique announced yesterday. Premier Golda Meir has decided that such a discussion be held by the Cabinet as soon as she returns from London — and her decision was announced to the ministers at a Cabinet meeting yesterday by her Deputy, Yigal Allon.

The army, meanwhile, is going ahead with its own inquiries into the war. Chief of Staff David Elazar told the Cabinet that such inquiries were the accepted practice after a war, and indeed after every action in which Zahal was involved.

They would cover the preparations for the war, the army's state of preparedness, the battles themselves and the tactics employed, he said. The purpose of the inquiries, the Chief of Staff said, would be to ascertain facts and to facilitate the learning of lessons and the drawing of conclusions on the organizational and theoretical level.

Attorney-General Meir Shamgar also pointed out that the army's inquiries need not in any way prejudice or bar any investigation or inquiry that may be decided on by the Cabinet.

(Among the proposals which have been raised — and are due to be discussed by the Cabinet — are for a judicial inquiry to be established under a judge, or for an inquiry by a panel including non-political representatives of the public, non-political public figures.)

(Related stories on pages 3 and 5.)

Bourguiba message to Gaddafi

TUNIS (Reuter). — Tunisian Foreign Minister Mohammed Masmoudi returned home yesterday after visiting Tripoli to hand a message from President Habib Bourguiba to Libyan leader Muammer Gaddafi.

Mr. Masmoudi said on arrival here that Col. Gaddafi was not opposed to an Arab summit following yesterday's signature by Israel and Egypt of an American-sponsored document aimed at stabilising the Middle East cease-fire, but wanted Arabs to bide their time.

There have been reports that an Arab summit would be held in Algiers before any Israel-Arab peace conference took place.

WATERGATE

Nixon to meet all Congressmen

NEW YORK. — Senator Charles H. Percy (Republican-Illinois) said yesterday that every member of Congress has been invited to meet with President Nixon in six unusual sessions this week to discuss the Watergate case.

"At least nine hours will be spent by the President being interrogated by members of the Congress, explaining his position," Percy said on a TV programme.

Percy said he believes that to restore public confidence the President must make "total and complete disclosure" of the Watergate documents with "nothing held back."

There must be "direct access by the special prosecutor, without a court order, for all documentation he feels is relevant and necessary" including material related to political donations, the ITT case, operations of the plumber's unit and the President's personal finances, Percy said.

"Anything related to the possibility of criminal activity should and must be revealed," Percy said. "I think the President is prepared to do this now."

Meanwhile, Eugene J. McCarthy, the former U.S. Senator who sought the 1968 presidential nomination as a Democratic candidate, said yesterday he saw no need to remove the President from office.

(AP, UPI)

Golda: Europe stand 'Munich attitude'

By DAVID LENNON
Jerusalem Post Correspondent

LONDON. — Prime Minister Golda Meir shocked the delegates to the Socialist International Executive into stunned silence yesterday afternoon, with the force of her attack on their countries' "Munich attitude" towards Israel during the past month.

Delivering the opening address, Mrs. Meir said she understood Europe's worries about oil; but that did not excuse their refusal to let U.S. supply planes use European air bases.

She was also able to understand the behaviour of Chamberlain at Munich, she said, but pointed out that this had not helped in the long run. Neither will last Tuesday's resolution of the EEC Foreign Ministers help Europe in the long run, she declared.

During her 55-minute address, Mrs. Meir spoke of the tragic loss of life in Israel and pointed out that the number of Israelis killed was proportionately equal to two and a half times the U.S. losses in 10 years of the war in Vietnam.

Golda Meir said this was a war of the few against the many. "It is not good to be small and alone," she concluded.

Amid a stunned silence, conference chairman Bruno Pitterman of Austria asked who would like to speak next. There were no takers. Then the Prime Minister of Mauritius, Sir Seewoosagur Ramgoolam, said Israel was not the only small country present and that he could not understand the Israeli Premier's reference to Munich. However, no other delegate was ready to speak, so the meeting had an unscheduled 20-minute adjournment.

It became clear in the discussion after the recess that there would be little possibility of an agreed resolution emerging from the meeting. This was mainly because of the stand of Premier Dom Mintoff of Malta and the Mauritius Prime Minister, who both took what Harold Wilson described as "a line markedly different" from other participants.

The differences of opinion which emerged led the delegates to decide to carry discussions on during and after the official dinner, which had been intended to celebrate the conclusion of the session.

After the conference, it was clear that different interpretations regarding responsibility for the Middle East situation still separated the various speakers.

There was general agreement on the need for vigilance and care to turn the fragile cease-fire into a peace settlement. Many of the participants expressed the view that boundaries must be a subject for negotiation. This included the future of East Jerusalem. It was pointed out that U.N. Security Council resolution 338, which called for the implementation of 242, also calls for negotiations between Israel and her Arab neighbours.

The delegates expressed their full support for the principle of negotiation.

Discussion of the EEC resolution of last week found most of the EEC representatives trying to interpret it in its most favourable light for Israel, noting that it called for secure and recognized boundaries for Israel.

The highlight of Premier Meir's round of meetings in London today will be her meeting with Prime Minister Edward Heath at 10 Downing Street, scheduled for 2 p.m.

Shortly after her arrival on Saturday night, Mrs. Meir conferred on tactics with Labour Party leader Harold Wilson, who is host to the conference. During nearly two hours of talks they sought a way of neutralizing the danger presented by the anti-Israel bloc led by Dom Mintoff of Malta and Mauritius Premier Ramgoolam.

Austrian Premier Bruno Kreisky let it be known in discussions with journalists earlier that he did not think there was any real need for the emergency meeting. As there had already been a cease-fire, he said, the subject of the Middle East should be discussed in the framework of the European security conference.

The meeting was attended by 39 participants from 20 countries. With the exception of Denmark (in the midst of a constitutional crisis), all the Prime Ministers who had promised to come did arrive.

An unexpected visitor to the conference hotel yesterday morning was former U.S. Vice-President Hubert Humphrey. In London on private business, he insisted on meeting with his "friends," including Golda Meir.

The formal session yesterday afternoon was followed by a dinner at which the lobbying was expected to remain intense, with Mrs. Meir being anxious to use every moment available to persuade the Europeans that it is not in their interest to appease the Arabs.

Complaint to IRC on PoW murders

Jerusalem Post Diplomatic Correspondent

Israel submitted a formal complaint to the International Red Cross over the weekend concerning the cold-blooded killing of Israeli prisoners of war. The IRC — which does not itself investigate complaints — will pass on the complaint to Syria.

The complaint refers to 28 proven cases of the murder of prisoners. The 28 bodies were found in four separate places on the Golan, with their hands tied behind their backs.

Sign Number Twenty-One

Comprehensive Middle East Peace Treaty

> And he shall confirm the covenant with many for one week: and in the midst of the week he shall cause the sacrifice and the oblation to cease. . . .
>
> —Daniel 9:27

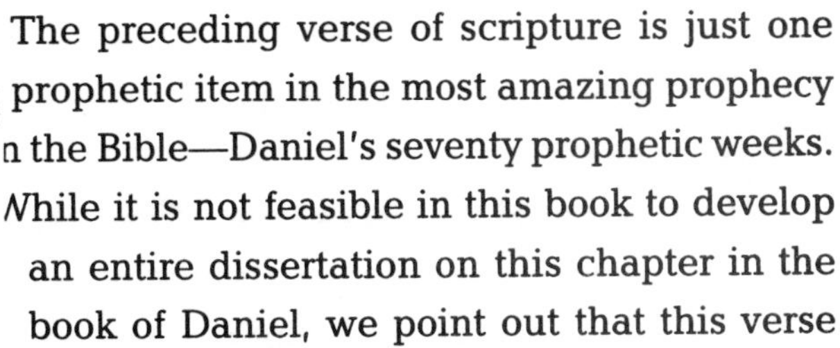

The preceding verse of scripture is just one prophetic item in the most amazing prophecy in the Bible—Daniel's seventy prophetic weeks. While it is not feasible in this book to develop an entire dissertation on this chapter in the book of Daniel, we point out that this verse relates to the last week, or the last seven years of this age that precede the messianic age. The most common, and we might add the most logical, explanation of this verse entails the concluding of a peace treaty with Israel in which some person will have the political and ecclesiastical authority to confirm "the covenant" with Israel.

No person, government, or international authority has to develop "the covenant." The "covenant" has been in existence since God promised Abraham the land of Canaan (Genesis 13:12–14) and all the land the children of Israel walked over (Deuteronomy 11:24). The Bible in many places indicates that some international figure will have the authority to promise security to Israel in their land. This prophecy is most important, because seven years from the time this confirmation occurs the Messiah will come. Again, Christians believe the Messiah is Jesus Christ who will come again. Orthodox Jewry believes their Messiah will come the first time, and they do not know who this Messiah will be.

To bring peace to Israel and a confirmation of "the covenant" that God made with the nation has been among the most difficult of world problems, but the Bible foretells this would be so. These are just a few of the steps that are leading to the fulfillment of Daniel 9:27; 12:11; Matthew 24:15–21:

- The Balfour Declaration—November 2, 1917
- The Mandate for Palestine—July 24, 1922
- U.N. General Assembly Resolution 181—November 29, 1947
- Declaration of the Establishment of the State of Israel—May 14, 1948
- Protection of Holy Places Law—June 27, 1967
- The Khartoum Resolutions—September 1, 1967
- U.N. Security Council Resolution 242—November 22, 1967
- U.N. Security Council Resolution 338—October 22, 1973
- Separation of Forces Agreement between Israel and Syria—May 31, 1974
- U.N. Security Council Resolution 425—March 19, 1978
- Camp David Accord—September 17, 1978
- Peace treaty between Israel and Egypt—March 26, 1979

- Basic law: Jerusalem, capital of Israel—July 30, 1980
- Golan Heights Law—December 14, 1981
- Israel's Peace Initiative—May 14, 1989
- Madrid Peace Conference—October 30, 1991
- Israel-PLO Recognition—September 9, 1993
- Israel-Palestinian Declaration of Principles—September 13, 1993 (Oslo Accord)
- Israel-Jordan Common Agenda—September 14, 1993
- Agreement on Gaza Strip and Jericho—May 4, 1994
- Washington Declaration (Israel–Jordan–U.S.),July 25, 1994
- Agreement on Transfer of Powers (Israel–PLO)—August 25, 1994
- Peace treaty between Israel and Jordan—October 26, 1994
- Interim agreement between Israel and Palestinians—September 28, 1995

Former Israeli prime minister Yitzhak Rabin and Palestine Liberation Organization chairman Yasser Arafat shake hands after signing a peace accord on the South Lawn of the White House, as President Clinton watches.

- Summit of Peacemakers (Sharm el-Sheikh)—March 13, 1996
- Israel–Lebanon ceasefire—April 26, 1996
- Agreement on Temporary International Presence in Hebron—May 9, 1996
- The Wye River Memorandum—October 23, 1998

The preceding is only a partial list of the efforts to bring peace between Israel and its neighbors. Yet, there is no peace. In fact, peace for Israel appears to grow further and further away.

Yasser Arafat, chairman of the Palestinian Authority, has internationally announced that a Palestinian state with East Jerusalem as its capital would be declared on May 4, 1999. Whether this was simply posturing or not cannot be determined at the writing of this book. Hillary Clinton, wife of President Clinton, has championed a Palestinian state in 1998. We have observed that if Mrs. Clinton so fervently wants to give a part of Israel for a Palestinian state, then let her give Chairman Arafat a state—her state, Arkansas.

At the writing of this book, the United States is providing the majority of the firepower to attack Yugoslavia over Kosovo, because as President Clinton announced, "Milosevic has failed to submit to the will of the international community." The operation in Yugoslavia is an operation dictated by the European Union with NATO forces to carry out the military efforts. As a member of NATO, the U.S. claims a legal right to be involved.

While this information may be dating this book, it is necessary to include because a CNN report of March 26, 1999, in headlines to a news story stated: **EU Supports Palestinian Statehood—Israel Given One-Year Deadline.**

> The European Union on Friday issued its strongest support yet for Palestinian statehood, which drew angry criticism

> from Israel and praise from the Palestinians. The statement, issued by EU leaders at a summit in Berlin of the fifteen-nation bloc, gave Israel a one-year deadline for fulfilling the "unqualified Palestinian right" to independence.

What if Israel does not submit to the will of the "international community"? On May 4, 2000, will NATO armies, U.N. armies, and U.S. armies be bombing Jerusalem and fighting in Israel? We certainly are not saying that this will happen, but the possibility is fraught with prophetic apprehension. In the same news story from CNN, Prime Minister Benjamin Netayahu is quoted in reference to a Palestinian state on the West Bank:

> Such a state would be able to raise a large army, use it without limitations, forge alliances with regimes that aim to destroy Israel, and serve as a base of increased terrorism against Israel, and in that way threaten its existence.

All the peace efforts, along with the signs of impending war more serious than any previous war, are serious and important messianic signs, because according to Zechariah before the Messiah comes, God will "gather all nations against Jerusalem to battle." But the good news for Israel is, "shall the Lord go forth, and fight against those nations, as when he fought in the day of battle."

Again, we cannot say for sure how near or how far in the future this event will be. However, considering all the other messianic signs in Israel, we need to be ready for the coming of the Lord at any time.

▪ ▪ ▪ ▪ ▪

One of the most controversial deterents to peace in the Middle East is the Temple Mount. When Israel captured the Temple

Mount during the 1967 war, Israeli soldiers did put a flag of Israel on top of Mount Moriah. Moshe Dayan gave orders to have it removed. Subsequently, the control of the Temple Mount was turned over to the Moslem Authority. Of course, Palestinian guards continue to control the traffic on the Mount. There have been incidents of Bibles being taken away from tourists; the Temple Mount Faithful group has attempted to lay a Temple foundation stone; and there have been more serious incidents when dozens have been killed. Unless there is some solution to the ownership of the Temple Mount, it is difficult to understand how there can be peace.

Of course, the plans announced by the Palestinian Authority to establish an independent Palestinian nation on the West Bank, whether this attempt is made this year or the next, is a real problem in any attempt to bring a peace arrangement between Israel and the Arab nations. When Israelites are asked about peace, they think about giving a piece of Israel for this or a piece of Israel for that. In addition to the problem of a Palestinian entity in Israel, there is an even greater problem in Mr. Arafat's ambition to make East Jerusalem the capital of this new Arab nation. And now we have all this external pressure from the United States, the United Nations, and the European Union, telling Israel what Israel must do.

Doubtless, the so-called peace process will continue, and there may even be a temporary peace arrangement, but we do not think there will be true peace until Messiah comes.

—Gilla

Sign Number Twenty-Two

The Closed Eastern Gate

> Then he brought me back the way of the gate of the outward sanctuary which looketh toward the east; and it was shut. Then said the LORD unto me; This gate shall be shut, it shall not be opened, and no man shall enter in by it; because the LORD, the God of Israel, hath entered in by it, therefore it shall be shut. It is for the prince; the prince, he shall sit in it to eat bread before the LORD; he shall enter by the way of the porch of that gate, and shall go out by the way of the same.
>
> —Ezekiel 44:1–3

The forty-fourth chapter of Ezekiel clearly gives a description of the Messianic Temple and the requirements for the priests to minister in this Temple, which the Messiah Himself will build. The verses quoted referred to the closing of the Eastern Gate. The tourist can look over the Temple Mount from the Mount of Olives and see quite plainly that the Eastern Gate is closed.

When the remnant from the Babylonian captivity era returned to rebuild Jerusalem, the wall, and the Temple, they built within the wall a gate on the east side, just on the west bank of the Brook Kidron, opposite the Garden of Gethsemane. This wall was torn down at the conclusion of the Roman siege of Jerusalem in A.D. 70. During the next fifteen hundred years various efforts were made to rebuild the wall, but then other invaders would tear the wall down. The wall with the Eastern Gate today was built by Suleiman the Magnificent in 1542 after the Ottoman Turks had conquered most of the Middle East. After the wall had been completed, Suleiman discovered that the surveyors and architects had failed-to extend the wall around Mount Zion, so he had them all beheaded.

Within the last decade the Eastern Gate of the wall that the Romans destroyed was discovered a few feet below the present gate. At the time of Jesus Christ, this gate was probably also called the Beautiful Gate, or the Golden Gate. This following information is taken from page 658 of the *Zondervan Pictorial Encyclopedia of the Bible:*

> **Gate, The Beautiful.** A gate in Herod's Temple, q.v. Whereas the "Beautiful Gate" of the NT Temple is known only from Acts 3, the phrase prob. refers to that entrance way, famous for its imported Corinthian bronze doors, which was the only E gate from the surrounding Court of the Gentiles into the Court of the Women (Jos. War. V. 5. 3). It was once identified with the single E gate that led from the Kidron Valley, through the outer wall and "Solomon's Porch," into the Court of the Gentiles—a fact that may account for the name of the later entrance way, not itself sealed up, that was built over it and called "Porta Aurea," the "Golden Gate." After Pentecost, a man lame from his mother's womb was laid daily at the Beautiful Gate to ask for alms, and was miraculously healed by Peter and John in the name of Jesus Christ (Acts 3:2, 10).

When Jesus was in Jerusalem he lodged with Mary, Martha, and Lazarus in Bethany. The obvious route from Bethany to

View of the Eastern Gate from the Garden of Gethsemane

the Temple would have been over the Mount of Olives, through the Garden of Gethsemane, and entry by the Eastern Gate. Some may contend that Jesus would not have gone through this gate because it was adjacent to the Court of the Women and the Court of the Gentiles. However, it is obvious from Acts chapter three that Peter and John used this gate, and up until Acts chapter ten Peter was careful not to defile himself with Gentile associations. Inasmuch as Jesus had fellowship with Mary and Martha, and sat down with publicans and Samaritans, it is quite probable that He would not have had an aversion to going through the Eastern Gate. We would also think that the Jewish builders of this gate would not have used such beautiful workmanship for only Gentile use.

It is not known exactly why the Eastern Gate was sealed. The explanation most often given is that Suleiman wanted better security measures imposed to keep Jews, Christians, and others considered by the Moslems as heathens, from going on the Temple Mount and "defiling" the Moslem shrine. It is also possible that Suleiman had heard of the Jewish prophecy that the Messiah would come through this gate, so he sealed it with heavy rock and concrete blocks. From Ezekiel 44:3 the subject continues to cover the worship and service of the priests and Levites who would go through the Eastern Gate into the Temple after the Messiah had opened it, and we read in verse twenty-five, "And they shall come at no dead person to defile themselves . . ." (except immediate family members). To be doubly sure, evidently, that the Messiah would not come through the Eastern Gate, the Moslems put a cemetery in front of it.

As an added further precaution that no Jew or Gentile will even get near the gate, the Jordanians have placed a Moslem guard on the inside. We have been able to tip the guard with five or ten dollars to allow us to take pictures of the inside of the gate. Nevertheless, the sealed Eastern Gate is another sign today that Israel awaits the coming of the messianic age.

▪ ▪ ▪ ▪ ▪

The Eastern Gate indeed remains absolutely shut. In Jewish tradition it is called "the gate of mercy." We believe that this gate is the gate through which the Messiah will come. I have heard that in 1967 King Hussein intended to open the Eastern Gate to make more room for the Moslems to enter the Temple Mount for prayers at the Dome of the Rock, or the El Aqsa Mosque. But just before the king could get around to opening the gate, the 1967 war occurred, so the gate remained sealed. The gate has been sealed now for almost seven hundred years. This particular gate preceded the complete restoration of the wall by Suleiman. But the sealed Eastern Gate remains as a promise to Israel that the Messiah must come and open it.

—Gilla

Sign Number Twenty-Three

The Dead Sea

> Arise, shine; for thy light is come, and the glory of the LORD is risen upon thee. . . . Gentiles shall come to thy light, . . . thy sons shall come from far. . . . Then thou shalt see . . . the abundance of the sea shall be converted unto thee, the forces of the Gentiles shall come unto thee.
>
> —Isaiah 60:1, 3–5

In this chapter the prophet foretells the blessing of God upon Israel during the messianic age when the riches of the Gentiles will come to the nation, and even the abundance of the sea will be converted to them. I have often remarked to the tour members of my group that they should not complain about high prices in Israel, because they are only helping to fulfill prophecy. Many have taken Isaiah's reference to the "sea" in this scripture to mean the Dead Sea, but this is an option rather than a definitive interpretation of the text. It could refer only to the Dead Sea, but it seems a more accurate interpretation within the context would be all major oceans and seas. It is also claimed by some that the wealth of the Dead Sea is more than all the wealth of the entire world combined, but we have difficulty understanding how the wealth of the world could be computed.

It seems that the Dead Sea did not play an important role in biblical history. Amaziah killed ten thousand Edomites in the Valley of Salt at the southern end of the Dead Sea. David and his men took refuge at the canyon oasis of Ein Gedi on the western shore of the Dead Sea. Sodom and Gomorrah were evidently located on a plain that once comprised the southern half of this area.

Josephus made reference to Roman soldiers making sport of throwing prisoners from cliffs into the "Asphaltic Sea." The poor captives would think they were going to be drowned, but they would only sink a foot or two into the heavily salt and mineral waters and then bob back up to the surface. The Dead Sea was called the Asphaltic Sea at the time of Jesus because huge amounts of oil would collect and semi-solidify on the surface. Romans and Jews would take the asphalt and pitch ships. We also read in the fourteenth chapter of Genesis that the kings of Sodom and Gomorrah and most of their armies were killed in the Vale of Siddim where there were many slime pits (bitumin, or oil pools). Hammurabi led the opposing forces, composed of the alliance of the kings of the north. There have been consider-

Salt and bromide pillars rising from the Dead Sea

able explorations for oil in the Dead Sea area, but the Dead Sea is a part of the largest earthquake fault in the world, the Syrian-African rift, which seriously complicates drilling efforts.

The Dead Sea is so named because nothing is said to live in its waters, although in recent years a subbiological entity has been found to exist in it. A few forms of plant life around the shores of the Dead Sea have also developed a tolerance to the heavy salt and mineral water. Water in the Dead Sea has a consistency of ten-weight motor oil, and it is true that it is impossible for people to sink.

The Dead Sea is approximately fifty miles long and ten miles wide. Its principal water source is the Jordan River. Because both Israel and Jordan now use most of the water of the river, the Dead Sea water level has been lowering by approximately a foot a year. Because of the drop in the water level, a land bridge now cuts off the southern one-third of the Dead Sea, and the heavily laden mineral waters are now channeled to the Sodom mineral and potash works through a canal.

Jesus referred to the signs of His return as the days of Sodom (Luke 17:28–30). Sodom has been restored as a city; and although it is principally a community for the mineral plant works, if you were to address a letter to the postmaster of Sodom, Israel, he would get it.

The Dead Sea is the lowest place on earth, one thousand three hundred twenty feet below sea level. According to a science report taken off the Internet (*www.extremescience.com/DeadSea.htm*), some places in the Dead Sea are twenty-three hundred feet deep and dropping, getting twenty-three inches a year deeper. The reason for this is that the Syrian-African rift that runs through the Red Sea, through the Arava under the Dead Sea, and then northward to Syria, is getting wider by the year. Geologists are warning about a possible second volcanic eruption.

At the same time, one side of the rift is shifting to the north and the other side to the south. This could allow water from the Mediterranean Sea to run down through the Jezreel Valley to the Jordan River south of the Sea of Galilee and then into the Dead Sea.

The waters from the Dead Sea are channeled to the mineral works at Sodom to remove valuable chemicals and fertilizers. The Dead Sea is a valuable source of income to Israel, but according to Ezekiel, there will come a time when this source of income will be no more, or at least be diminished. Ezekiel wrote about the future of the Dead Sea in the messianic age:

> And it shall come to pass, that the fishers shall stand upon it from Engedi even unto Eneglaim; they shall be a place to spread forth nets; their fish shall be according to their kinds, as the fish of the great sea, exceeding many. But the miry places thereof and the marishes thereof shall not be healed; they shall be given to salt.
>
> —Ezekiel 47:10–11

From the land bridge across the Dead Sea near Engedi, all the way to the northern end of the Dead Sea, the waters will be as the waters of the Great Sea, or the Mediterranean Sea. Fish from the Mediterranean will come down into this section of the Dead Sea. The area south of the land bridge today evidently will remain salty. It would appear that will be a huge geological change in this area. Evidence based on the geological activity today along the Syrian-African rift would indicate another huge earthquake like the one that occurred in A.D. 749.

It is also amazing that for the past twenty years Israel has considered building a canal from the Mediterranean Sea to the Dead Sea. This would possibly fulfill the prophecy of Ezekiel, but due to Israel having so many problems and lack of funds for the project, it has been put on hold.

Nevertheless, the movements of the Syrian-African rift along with Israeli plans for the Med-Dead Canal, can be considered another messianic sign of things to come in the land of the Bible.

▪ ▪ ▪ ▪ ▪

The riches of the Dead Sea are indeed incredible. Israel has virtually no other natural resources. Golda Meir used to joke that the reason it took Moses forty years to reach the Promised Land was that he looked for the one place that didn't have oil! Many believe that oil will be discovered one day in Israel, but so far none has been found in commercial quantities.

The Dead Sea is a very important source of minerals. Asphalt is a side product of the petrol industry, therefore in its synthetic form asphalt is plentiful in modern days. In antiquity asphalt was scarce and the Dead Sea was a major source for it. The Egyptians used asphalt in large quantities in the fourteenth century B.C. for mummifying. Like in ships, it was used to cover houses along the Nile and make them impermeable during floods. The Egyptians used asphalt to protect storehouses and precious objects. The medical qualities of asphalt were well known, and indeed it has quasi-antiobiotic properties. In the Hellenistic period the Nabateans were the unquestioned traders in asphalt. They would mine it, ship it on the Dead Sea, and then sell it. Alexander Janeus the Hasmonean king took the trade over. The Romans were familiar with the cosmetic qualities of the water of the Dead Sea and were will-

ing to pay good money for this water.

Theodore Herzl, founder of the Zionist movement, understood the potential in the Dead Sea both for the minerals and also for hydroelectric energy. The big elevation of the mountains near the sea, almost fifteen hundred feet, and the possibility of bringing water and creating a tall waterfall caught his eye right away. This indeed would be one of the main purposes of the Dead Sea Canal. The most recent version of it would bring the water from the Red Sea rather than the Mediterranean.

In 1911 Alexander Novomeiski, a Zionist mine engineer, came to Israel from Siberia, first as a tourist. He took samples of Dead Sea water to his lab, and returned as an immigrant in 1920. In 1925 he set up an experimental station on the northwest coast and tried extracting minerals by evaporation. The Zionist organization negotiated for many years, first with the Turks and then with the British, for a concession to mine the Dead Sea minerals. It was finally obtained in 1930, and then Novomeiski could move right away to start building a plant. A year later he was already producing bromine, and then potash. Needing more space for evaporating pools, he prepared large pools in the south and a second plant was built. Its production soon surpassed that of the northern one. This became the "Potash Company," and during World War II it supplied eighty percent of the potash consumption of Great Britain.

The 1948 war of independence was rough on the Dead Sea industry. The northern plant remained in Jordan, and the southern one had to be completely reorganized, as it was based on cooperation with Jordan in its water supply and manpower. "Dead Sea Works" (DSW) was formed and it is now part of Israel Chemical Industries, the sixteenth largest industry in the country. It employs thousands of workers and exports its products to over fifty countries.

The potash division produces and markets potash products in a variety of grades and qualities. Potash, along with nitrogen and phosphorous, is one of the essential ingredients for plant growth. In 1997 potash production equaled the previous year's record production of 2.48 million tons. New markets were developed and sales were increased to existing markets in China, India, and Brazil. A new investment program in 1999 is expected to increase production capacity by two hundred fifty thousand tons per year.

Dead Sea Magnesium, a joint venture between DSW (sixty-five percent) and Volkswagen (thirty-five percent) cast 7.2 tons of magnesium metal in 1977, the company's first year of operations. DSM is attempting to lower costs and increase production. In 1999 production should reach thirty-three thousand tons. Global magnesium consumption was three hundred thirty thousand tons in 1997, and demand for magnesium cast components by the automotive industry is expected to increase. The chemical division produces a variety of products extracted from the Dead Sea, including magnesium chloride flakes and pellets, aluminum chloride, and various salt grades including table salt. Raw materials for the cosmetic industry are also produced, and the division is responsible for the Clearon Corp., which produces chlorine-based products for water purification. Dead Sea Laboratories (Ahava) manufactures cosmetics. The company's sales revenues for 1997 amounted to $453 million, an increase of twenty-seven percent over the previous year. DSW's net income for 1997 was $39.6 million. Earnings per share amounted to $0.14 in 1997. The operating cost for DSW without subsidiaries was $73 million in 1997, compared to $63 million in 1996.

The wealth of the Dead Sea is being connected to the preparation of Israel for the Messiah.

1979

MARCH

Su	Mo	Tu	We	Th	Fr	Sa
				1	2	3
4	5	6	7	8	9	10
11	12	13	14	15	16	17
18	19	20	21	22	23	24
25	26	27	28	29	30	31

1. China agrees to pay 41 cents on the dollar for U.S. assets seized in 1949 (→ 1/24/80).

4. Uganda: Invading Tanzanian forces near capital (→ 29).

7. U.S. sends arms and advisers to North Yemen (→ 1/24/86).

9. Milwaukee: U.S. judge bars use of article on how to build H-bomb (→ 4/6).

9. N.H.: Hundreds protest delivery of reactor at Seabrook nuclear power plant (→ 13).

11. Washington: Andres Segovia performs at White House.

13. Washington: NRC orders five atomic plants shut (→ 28).

13. Grenada: Socialist Maurice Bishop seizes power in coup (→ 2/24/82).

18. N.J.: 20 tons hashish seized in largest bust in U.S. history.

20. Israel: Begin bars Palestinian state in occupied area (→ 26).

21. Washington: Report Mary Leakey has discovered world's oldest known biped footprints.

22. The Hague: British Ambassador to Netherlands Richard Sykes is slain.

23. Nevada: Larry Holmes retains title with TKO of Osvaldo Ocasio in seventh round.

26. Utah: Michigan State beats Indiana State for NCAA basketball title.

26. Washington: Begin and Sadat sign formal treaty, ending 30 years of war (→ 27).

27. Baghdad: Arab League agrees on steps against Egypt for signing of peace treaty (→ 31).

28. Britain: Callaghan Labor government ousted by vote in Commons (→ 5/3).

28. Pennsylvania: Accident at Three Mile Island reactor releases radiation (→ 30).

30. Iran: Referendum establishes 98% support for Islamic Republic (→ 4/7).

30. Washington: NRC reports danger of meltdown at Three Mile Island (→ 31).

DEATH

16. Jean Monnet, French architect of EEC (*11/9/1888).

Egypt, Israel sign treaty

Sadat, Carter and Begin enjoy a moment of triumph at the White House.

March 31. Egypt's President Anwar el-Sadat has made history by signing a peace treaty with Israel. He has also managed to isolate himself in the Arab world. The foreign ministers of 18 Arab countries moved in Baghdad today to cut diplomatic and economic relations with Cairo. Their agreement was also approved by the Palestine Liberation Organization. It calls for the immediate recall of ambassadors from Egypt, a complete termination of diplomatic relations within a month, an end to all financial aid and the imposition of economic sanctions. Egypt receives a billion dollars a year from other Arab countries, mainly Saudi Arabia.

Sadat indicated he was aware of the risks when he signed the peace agreement with Israel's Prime Minister Begin at the White House on Monday. Sadat also recognized its historic importance, and he praised President Carter for his role in masterminding the accord. "Without any exaggeration, what he did constitutes one of the greatest achievements of our time," Sadat said.

Sadats and Carters at Pyramids.

Carter, who signed the agreement as a witness, said it proved that "peace has come." Carter also said, "We have won, at last, the first step of peace, a first step on a long and difficult road."

Just how long and difficult it will be was clear in the remarks of Prime Minister Begin. He said the agreement meant "no more war, no more bloodshed, no more bereavement." But Begin also indicated he will resist a key demand from Sadat to relinquish control over eastern Jerusalem. The Israeli prime minister spoke emotionally of the day "when Jerusalem became one city and our brave, perhaps most hardened soldiers, the parachutists, embraced with tears and kissed the ancient stones of the remnants of the wall destined to protect the chosen place of God's glory."

The Israeli-Egyptian agreement took months to negotiate, and diplomats worked past midnight on the day it was signed to finalize the language. The last stumbling block was the timetable for Israeli withdrawal from oil fields in the Sinai. Sadat and Begin agreed they would be returned to Egypt seven months after the treaty is ratified (→ 4/2).

Sign Number Twenty-Four

The Remnant of Edom

> In that day will I raise up the tabernacle of David that is fallen, and close up the breaches thereof; and I will raise up his ruins, and I will build it as in the days of old: That they may possess the remnant of Edom. . . .
>
> —Amos 9:11–12

Within the context of prophetic overview of Israel's return to the land, and the preparations of both the people and the land for the Millennial Kingdom, Amos inserted a seemingly insignificant reference to the "remnant of Edom."

In the biblical record we read that Esau and Jacob were twins, but in the womb before they were born, God loved Jacob and hated Esau (Romans 9:13; Malachi 1:1–3). The attitude of God toward the twin brothers was based upon what they would become and how their descendants would be included in His eternal plan and purpose. After Esau despised his birthright and traded it to Jacob, he established his kingdom in Edom. Edom comprised the southern one-third of what today is Jordan. The inhabitants of this country at the time were called Horites, and

Tourists riding through Petra

Esau chased them out of the regions of Mount Hor, or Mount Seir. *Edom* means "red" and *Seir* means "hairy," both descriptions typical of Esau's nature.

In Edom there was a rugged area, approximately thirty-two square miles, adjacent to Mount Hor of caves and landlocked canyons, accessible only through a narrow gorge of twenty to fifty feet. The walls on either side of the narrow gorge are five to seven hundred feet high, making it difficult for invaders to capture this cavern city. It is thought that it was here that Job established his estate in the "land of Uz" (Job 1:1). It also seems evident that the apostle Paul took refuge here after his escape from Damascus. The city that became the capital of Esau's kingdom was later called Petra (rock) by the Greeks. The entire complex, including Biatra and Little Petra, comprises an area of one hundred thirty square miles. When the descendants of Jacob were in Egypt for four hundred years, the descendants of Esau likewise multiplied in Edom. When Moses asked for permission for the children of Israel to pass through Edom on the way to the Promised Land, not only did the king of Edom refuse, but sent out an army to attack the Israelites.

El Ciq—the entrance to Petra

The ancestral feud that existed between Esau and Jacob continued through their descendants. The biblical account of wars between Edom and Israel are numerous. However, the threat of the rising Babylonian Empire did result in a mutual assistance pact between Israel and Edom. Nevertheless, Edom betrayed Israel and actually joined Babylon in the destruction of Jerusalem and the Temple:

> By the rivers of Babylon, there we sat down, yea, we wept, when we remembered Zion. We hanged our harps upon the willows in the midst thereof. For there they that carried us away captive required of us a song; and they that wasted us required of us mirth, saying, Sing us one of the songs of Zion. How shall we sing the LORD's song in a strange land? If I forget thee, O Jerusalem, let my right hand forget her cunning. If I do not remember thee, let my tongue cleave to the roof of my mouth; if I prefer not Jerusalem above my chief joy. Remember, O LORD, the children of Edom in the day of Jerusalem; who said, Rase it, rase it, even to the foundation thereof.
>
> —Psalm 137:1–7

Carved buildings inside Petra

Racial mixing was one of the ways ancient conquerors would nationally weaken occupied territories. Under the Babylonian Empire, Israelites were moved to Babylon, and Edomites were moved into Israel. Subsequently, either of their own volition or under pressure from Babylon, the Nabateans moved into Petra. The Nabateans were descendants of Ishmael through his first son, Nabajoth. From 500 B.C. to

A.D. 500 the Nabateans enlarged their territories. However, the remnant of the Edomites continued in certain areas of Edom and Israel. When the Romans moved into this area, they called the Edomites Idumaeans or Edomeans (*Westminster Dictionary of the Bible,* 148). The Romans were more friendly toward the Idumaeans than the Jews. The Herods were Edomite puppet rulers. It would seem that without controversy, the Palestinians of today are largely Edomite, or Idumaean, descendants. The controversy today between the Jews and the Edomites is the same as indicated in Psalm 137.

The Edomite stronghold of Petra declined in importance after the Roman Empire broke up in about A.D. 500. Many began to doubt that such a city ever existed. Finally, in 1812 a Swiss explorer visited the city and news of its antiquity and beauty was reported to the world. Shortly afterward, Jews began returning to Israel. Today various Arab interests and the United Nations are busily restoring water sources, paving roads, and making it more accessible to Jews and Gentiles alike. A Jew could not visit Petra until 1995. In 1980 there was one hotel in Petra; in 1999 there were sixty-five hotels in Petra.

The Abomination of Desolation initially involves an attempt to kill the Jews living in the area of Jerusalem. While Daniel describes this act specifically in his book, Jesus further added:

> When ye therefore shall see the abomination of desolation, spoken of by Daniel the prophet, stand in the holy place, (whoso readeth, let him understand:) Then let them which be in Judaea flee into the mountains: . . . For then shall be great tribulation, such as was not since the beginning of the world to this time, no, nor ever shall be.
>
> —Matthew 24:15–16, 21

Of this time, the prophet Isaiah indicated that a remnant of Israel would be protected in a special place of chambers:

> Come, my people, enter thou into thy chambers, and shut thy doors about thee: hide thyself as it were for a little moment, until the indignation be overpast. For, behold, the LORD cometh out of his place to punish the inhabitants of the earth for their iniquity: the earth also shall disclose her blood, and shall no more cover her slain.
>
> —Isaiah 26:20–21

Petra is located in the highest mountain range in the area, approximately ten miles from the southern end of the Dead Sea. Mount Hermon is higher, but it is over two hundred miles to the north. There are dozens of prophetic references to a hiding place for a remnant of Israel during the "time of Jacob's trouble," also believed to be the last half of the Tribulation period. There are many indications within these scriptures that this hiding place will be the restored city of Petra. It appears more than coincidental that international agencies are now busily preparing Petra for it's future. Petra was known as a place of refuge—David found refuge here from Saul; Paul found refuge here to escape those who sought to kill him. The following prophecy indicates this city will be a place of refuge for Israel:

> O God, thou hast cast us off, thou hast scattered us, thou hast been displeased; O turn thyself to us again. . . . Who will bring me into the strong city? who will lead me into Edom? Wilt not thou, O God, which hadst cast us off? and thou, O God, which didst not go out with our armies? Give us help from trouble: for vain is the help of man. Through

> God we shall do valiantly: for he it is that shall tread down our enemies.
>
> —Psalm 60:1, 9–12

The continuing, unsolvable controversy between the descendants of Esau and the descendants of Jacob, along with current developments in Petra, is another strong messianic sign in Israel today.

Amos prophesied that in the last days Israel would possess the "remnant of Edom." There must be a remnant of Edom today, and the Palestinians in Israel must be the remaining descendants of Esau.

■ ■ ■ ■ ■

Petra is an unbelievable place. Those who have been there can't forget it. No wonder it fired the imagination of filmmakers and of explorers. After the peace agreement with Jordan in 1994, literally the whole of Israel ran to Petra.

In Israeli consciousness Petra occupies a special place. Until 1967 Israel was a very small country, even smaller than what it is now. For young Israelis with a keen sense of adventure and a desire to travel and hike, it was claustrophobic. The hardest aspect was that we couldn't go anywhere over land. Wherever we went, before we knew it, there was a sign, "STOP! Border Ahead!" Petra became a real subject of dream and fantasy. Several people would cross the border at night and sneak into Petra. Once the Jordanians learned of it, they would wait at the entrance to the Ciq and simply shoot them. The Ciq is the only access to this red city, carved in the rock.

Meir Har-Zion, Israel's legendary soldier and hero, devoted many pages in his journal to the trip he took to Petra in 1952 with a girlfriend—illegally crossing the border at the Ara-

va and then hiking into Petra. It took them seven days! A song was written called "The Red Rock." The song was very popular, but then it was banned. The authorities were afraid it would encourage more people to go to Petra.

Now Petra is quite easily accessible to Israelis. We can simply rent a car across the border and drive up there. Nevertheless, it still holds great interest and many Israelis like to go there.

When Brother Hutchings speaks to the tour group about Petra and how one day it will be a hiding place for a remnant of Israelis during the time of Jacob's trouble, I jokingly remark that when I went to Petra I picked out my own personal cave.

—Gilla

THE JERUSALEM POST

LATE EDITION 2.30 A.M.

IL7.00 (inc. Vat)

TUESDAY, MARCH 27, 1979 • ADAR 28, 5739 • RABI THANI 27, 1399 • VOL. XLIX, No. 14581

Israel and Egypt sign peace treaty declaring end to 30-year state of war

Begin, Sadat and Carter pledge shalom, salaam at White House ceremony

THE JERUSALEM POST

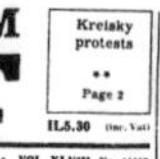
Kreisky protests

• •

Page 2

IL5.30 (inc. Vat)

WEDNESDAY, SEPTEMBER 6, 1978 • ELUL 4, 5738 • SHAWWAL 4, 1398 • VOL. XLVIII, No. 14413

Begin and Sadat arrive at Camp David for M.E. summit

President Carter greets President Sadat on arrival at Camp David yesterday afternoon. (UPI telephoto)

Sadat: Can't afford to fail at Camp David

Prime Minister Begin and President Carter embrace upon the premier's arrival at Camp David. (UPI telephoto)

First round of talks between Carter, Begin

THE JERUSALEM POST

Sunday, February 24, 1980 VOL. L, No. 14804 IL15.00

Shekel makes debut today; Gov't takes steps to fight 'black money'

THE JERUSALEM POST

3 a.m.

Wednesday, July 1, 1981 VOL. LI, No. 15265 IS 5.50

Labour and Likud in see-saw battle

THE JERUSALEM POST

Monday, October 24, 1983 Vol. LI, No. 15451

U.S. stunned by Beirut disaster

Reagan determined to continue with Lebanon objectives

146 Marines, 30 French killed; search for survivors goes on

THE JERUSALEM POST

Vol. LIII, No. 15802 Friday, January 4, 1985 • Tevet 11, 5745 • Rabia Tani 11, 1405 IS500

Arrival in Israel seen as miracle by new olim • Absorption centres, hotels and army facilities mobilized to house thousands • Hospitals treat for malnutrition and unusual ailments • Newcomers, some barefoot, arrive without possessions

Wraps off massive operation to rescue Jews of Ethiopia

Sign Number Twenty-Five

Jewish Unbelief

Along the interestate highways in the United States, signs inform motorists what restaurants, motels, or gas stations are available at the next exit. Sometimes two sets of signs might be in evidence should the motorist miss the first signs. However, what if there were twenty-five signs informing the motorists that at exit 215 there is a McDonalds?

In this book we present twenty-five messianic signs in Israel today that the coming of the Messiah is at the next exit. We would think that every Jew in the land of Israel would, therefore, be alertly and joyfully looking for the Messiah to appear at any time. Not exactly!

After leading thirty or more tours to Israel, it seems to me that most Jews do at least have an awareness that there is a reason why they are back in the land. They may not know the reason, and may even credit the existence of Israel out of the Diaspora as fate. Some observing Jews are discerning the signs of the time in reference to the Messiah's appearance, but their number is relatively few. The keeper at the gate to the Qumran archaeological site called out to my group on my last tour to Israel: "Do you Americans know that a red heifer has been born in Israel. This could be the tenth red heifer, and the Messiah will come when the tenth red heifer is sacrificed."

The apostle Paul observed in his first letter to the church at Corinth: "For the Jews require a sign, and the Greeks seek after wisdom" (1 Cor. 1:22). It is a common belief among pre-millennial Christian ministers that no sign of the end of the age is given to the Gentile church. I am not sure I agree with this conclusion, although I would certainly agree that the vast majority of Kingdom age signs are for the Jews. Therefore, Christians search the scriptures for messianic signs to the Jews to know when the end of the church age is in view.

There are over one hundred scriptures in the Bible where we read, "this shall be a sign unto you. . . ." Most of these scriptures are in reference to the messianic age. We read in Exodus 31:13 that keeping the sabbath (Saturday) holy as commanded in the Torah is a sign to Israel. A sign of what? Just counting McDonald's signs along the interstate is not going to get the motorist a Big Mac. Likewise, just keeping sabbath after sabbath is not going to bring the blessings of the messianic age, the millennial sabbath that is promised to Israel.

John the Baptist preached to Israel: "Repent, for the kingdom of heaven is near" (Matt. 3:2). Evidently, Israel never repented. Jesus said to Israel, "You will not see me again until you shall say, Blessed is he that cometh in the name of the Lord." It is obvious that Israel has not sent out an invitation for Jesus to come back. Peter and John even pleaded with Israel to call out to God to send Jesus back (Acts 3:19–20).

Maybe Israelis do not know what kind of a Messiah they want, or what they expect of him. I asked one prominent Zionist Jew why he did not believe that Jesus is the Messiah, and he replied: "Isaiah prophesied that the Messiah would be Immanuel, and I cannot believe in a God who had to use the bathroom." However, the prophet indicated the Messiah would be born of a virgin, a baby, and grow up among the people.

Most Jews I have discussed the Messiah with are looking for the same kind that the Jews of Jesus' day were seeking—a great leader who will defeat all of Israel's enemies and in the glory of the Lord bring all the blessings promised in the covenants. I asked another noted Jewish personality how a mere human, regardless of his political and ecclesiastical power, could do all of this. He had no acceptable response.

The late Dr. Maurice Jaffe, rabbi of Jerusalem Great Synagogue and president of the Israeli Assembly of Synagogues, when asked if Jesus could be the Messiah, replied, "When the Messiah comes, we will ask him."

Another well-known Israeli whom I asked recently had he ever considered that Jesus might be the Messiah, answered: "If I am around when the Messiah stands on Mount

Orthodox Jews in celebration at Wailing Wall. On Shabbat a divider is erected for division between genders—men on one side, women on the other

Olivet, the first thing I will ask is to see if there are nail prints in his hands."

Other Jews, when I have broached the subject, simply reply, "I can't believe that; I am a Jew."

Muslims in Israel also believe in a Messiah, and they call him Mahdi. Many Muslims believe that their Mahdi will be Jesus when He returns as a Muslims. They believe he will kill everyone on earth who does not convert to the Muslim religion.

Evangelical Christians may be confused and frustrated why some Jews do not love them as much as they love the Jews, or why Jews will not accept Jesus Christ as their Messiah, Lord, and Savior. However, the Jews have been persecuted and killed by the state church in Spain and even Protestants in Germany, Poland, Eastern Europe, and the Russian Orthodox Church in the Soviet Union. On a historical basis, the Jews have more reason to fear Christians than to love them. Nevertheless, today evangelical Christians are the best friends in the world that Israel has.

Basic Christian eschatology teaches us that Jesus will not come back until Israel is ready to accept Him as the Messiah, and this will occur only after the time that Daniel forewarned: ". . . a time of trouble, such as never was since there was a nation. . . ." (Daniel 12:1); and Jesus: ". . . then shall be great tribulation, such as was not since the beginning of the world to this time, no, nor ever shall be" (Matthew 24:21).

This we know according to Zechariah: the Messiah, King, the Lord of Hosts, will come . . . He will stand upon the Mount of Olives and Israel will mourn for Him as the one whom "they have pierced" (Zechariah 12:10). Christians believe this one whom Israel will behold as the Lord of hosts, will be Jesus Christ at His second coming. Jews who believe in the Messiah's coming await His identification.

When the Jews began returning at the turn of the century, most were secular (atheists or agnostics). These were the Jews who established the *kibbutzim* system. Most of the Jews in the *kibbutz* system are still nonreligious. To Israel's credit, students in state schools will have read the Torah through several times before graduating from the eighth grade.

According to the genealogy of Jesus in Matthew and Luke, He is a Jew from the lineage of David. The twelve apostles of Jesus were Jews. Until after Acts chapter ten, members of the early church were Jews. The split in the early church was when Paul of Tarsus, a student of Gamaliel, appeared in Damascus to announce his conversion to Christianity. Saul changed his name to Paul and also announced that God had given him an understanding of the gospel of Jesus Christ that would be for the salvation of the Gentiles. The Jews evidently were not impressed with the gospel that could save Gentiles, and so Paul at the end of his ministry concluded:

> For the heart of this people is waxed gross, and their ears are dull of hearing, and their eyes have they closed; lest they should see with their eyes, and hear with their ears, and understand with their heart, and should be converted, and I should heal them. Be it known therefore unto you, that the salvation of God is sent unto the Gentiles, and that they will hear it.
>
> —Acts 28:27–28

Peter and James twenty years earlier had presented the same evident truth:

> . . . God at the first did visit the Gentiles, to take out of them a people for his name. . . . After this I will return, and will build again the tabernacle of David, which is fallen down;

> and I will build again the ruins thereof, and I will set it up: That the residue of men might seek after the Lord, and all the Gentiles, upon whom my name is called, saith the Lord, who doeth all these things.
>
> —Acts 15:14, 16–17

▪ ▪ ▪ ▪ ▪

Jewish people are very aware of Messiah and expect him to come. Jews of faith pray daily and say, "I believe Messiah will come, and even though he tarries I will wait for him every day." To add one other aspect, I believe that Jews expect of Messiah what Christians expect of the second coming.

It is true that Jewish people find it hard to understand evangelical Christians. They have a constant feeling that Christians try to convert them, and I must confess that in my work with evangelical Christians it usually doesn't fail. In every group there is at least one who will give it a try . . .

Joking aside, those of us who work with evangelical Christians and who get to know them, are very well aware of the wonderful care and friendship toward Israel. We know that Christians make a very strong lobby in the U.S. politically, and we know we can always rely on them. There are lots of common values we share, especially in looking for a wholesome and healthy way of life for our families and ourselves.

—Gilla

▪ ▪ ▪ ▪ ▪

All down through the church age, probably no more than one percent of the Jews have converted to Christianity. Probably no more than one percent of the Jews in Israel today have converted to Christianity. It would also be a fair estimate that only about one-third of the Jews in the land today are earnestly seeking for God's will and observing the messianic signs evident in Israel today. However, the good news is:

> And I will bring the third part through the fire, and will refine them as silver is refined, and will try them as gold is tried: they shall call on my name, and I will hear them: I will say, It is my people: and they shall say, The LORD is my God. **Behold, the day of the LORD cometh. . . .**
>
> —Zechariah 13:9, 14:1

Pray for the peace of Jerusalem:
they shall prosper that love thee.

—Psalm 122:6